THE NORN LANGUAGE
OF ORKNEY &
SHETLAND

THE NORN LANGUAGE OF ORKNEY AND SHETLAND

MICHAEL P. BARNES

The Shetland Times Ltd.
Lerwick
1998

The Norn Language of Orkney and Shetland
Copyright © Michael P. Barnes, 1998.

ISBN 1 898852 29 4
First published by The Shetland Times Ltd., 1998.

Cover design by The Stafford Partnership, Shetland.

British Library Cataloguing-in-Publication Data
A catalogue record for this book is available from the British Library.

Printed and published by
The Shetland Times Ltd.,
Prince Alfred Street,
Lerwick, Shetland ZE1 0EP, UK.

CONTENTS

LIST OF ILLUSTRATIONS

PREFACE

This book provides an account of Norn — the Scandinavian language that was for some 800-900 years the vernacular of Orkney and Shetland. First, the origin and meaning(s) of the term 'Norn' are discussed. This leads in to a history of Scandinavian speech in the Northern Isles, taking the reader from the Viking settlement in the 800s to the replacement of Norn by Scots in the 1700s — and its aftermath. Attention is focused first on the settlement itself — its date and the place or places of origin of the settlers. There is then an examination of the linguistic situation in Orkney and Shetland prior to and following the arrival of the Norsemen — in as far as this is understood — leading to conjecture about what happened to the indigenous language or languages once a form of Scandinavian speech had become established. Next an attempt is made to trace the development of Norn through the somewhat scanty sources that have come down to us: runic inscriptions, documents written in the roman alphabet and records of the spoken language. There follows a detailed discussion of the demise of Norn: why did it die out, when, and in what circumstances? Finally, consideration is given to what remains of Norn today — the traces it has left in modern Orkney and Shetland dialect. This history is complemented by a survey of the principal features of Norn and a selection of texts with English translations and commentaries. Endnotes explain a number of concepts that may be unfamiliar to readers, and there is a full bibliography for those who wish to follow up particular aspects of the subject.

If a book of this nature is to avoid the danger of superficiality it must include a modicum of detail. Where required I have provided examples: as illustrations, as evidence in support of assertions and arguments, and — not least — to give readers a flavour of Northern-Isles Scandinavian at the different periods of its existence. Those who find the examples more of a hindrance than a help are advised to ignore them — at least in the first instance; they are not essential to a general understanding of Norn. A number of linguistic terms also make their appearance. It is unfortunately impossible to discuss language or languages fruitfully without them. Where I have felt that a term might be unfamiliar I have explained it in the endnotes. Any that are not covered there should be sought in a comprehensive English dictionary or, failing that, a specialist dictionary of linguistic terms, of which there are now several.

The present account of Norn is based on my paper: 'The origin, development and decline of Orkney and Shetland Norn', which appeared in *The Origins and Development of Emigrant Languages* (1996), edited by Hans F. Nielsen and Lene Schøsler and published by Odense University Press (*RASK* Supplement vol. 6, *NOWELE* Supplement vol. 17). I am grateful to Odense University Press for allowing me to present a revised and expanded version of the paper here.

Thanks are due to the Orkneymen, Shetlanders and others who have helped me in one way or another in the course of my research. To Brian Smith, the Shetland Archivist, I owe a particular debt of gratitude. He has followed my work with interest, challenged a number of my too-hasty conclusions, and provided me with much encouragement and many elusive pieces of information. Thanks must also go to *The Shetland Times* for so readily agreeing to publish this work and for making it such an attractive volume.

London, 1998

ABBREVIATIONS AND SYMBOLS

acc.	accusative
adj.	adjective
Dan.	Danish
dat.	dative
f.	feminine
Far.	Faroese
gen.	genitive
imp.	imperative
indic.	indicative
inf.	infinitive
m.	masculine
n.	neuter
nom.	nominative
ON	Old Norse (= Old Scandinavian)
pl.	plural
pres.	present
sg.	singular
subj.	subject/subjunctive
[ ]	phonetic transcription[1]
/ /	phonemic transcription[1]
:	indicates length in a sound or phoneme
< >	written form
>	develops to
<	develops from
*	reconstructed (assumed) form

PRONUNCIATION

The approximate sound values of International Phonetic Alphabet symbols and other special characters used in the book are:

ø	As French 'eu' in *peu*, or German 'ö' in *böse*.
œ	The same sound, but always long.
ɛ	As English 'e' in *let*, but can be short or long.
ǫ	As English 'o' in *hot* (Old Norse spelling).
ɔ	As English 'o' in *hot* (International Phonetic Alphabet notation).
æ	As English 'a' in *hat* or *man*.
ə	As English 'a' in *about*.
j	As English 'y' in *year*.
ʎ	Palatal *l*, pronounced with the tongue raised so that it touches the hard palate.
ɲ	Palatal *n*, pronounced with the same tongue position.
ð	As English 'th' in *father*.
þ	As English 'th' in *think*.

We cannot say in any detail how Norn pronunciation developed from its Old Norse origins. It is assumed that the vowels a, e, i, o, u, y had roughly their 'continental' values: a was like 'a' in English *father*, e like French 'é' in *été* or German 'e' in the first syllable of *lesen*, i like 'ea' in English *eat*, o like German 'o' in *los* and similar to 'oa' in the Scottish pronunciation of *coat*, u like French 'ou' in *bouche* or German 'u' in *suchen* and similar to 'oo' in English *cool*, y like French 'u' in *pur* or German 'ü' in *üben*. Vowels marked by an acute accent in Old Norse spelling were long equivalents of the corresponding short vowels, but in later forms of Scandinavian they often came to have different values from their short counterparts. There is evidence in <wo> and related spellings, for example, that at least in certain kinds of Norn ON *á* had become a diphthong, perhaps something like /ɔa/, the Faroese reflex of the same sound (see pp.17 and 20). The consonants of Norn probably did not differ markedly from their English equivalents. Worth noting is that written 'j' was pronounced like 'y' in English *year*, and that 'r' was almost certainly rolled as in many parts of Scotland. It is probable that *g* and *k* were pronounced with a following [j] sound before vowels such as /i/, /y/ and /e/, or even as 'dg' in English *ridge* (*g*) and 'ch' in English *church* (*k*). For further information on the phonology of Norn, see Barnes 1984:357-9; Jakobsen 1928-32:xliv-lix; Marwick 1929:xxxix-xlvii.

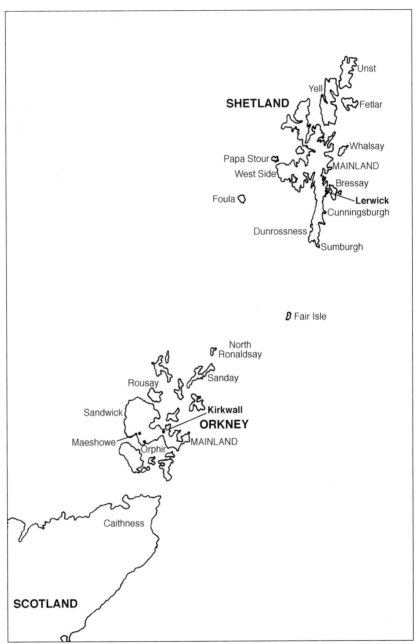

Orkney and Shetland.

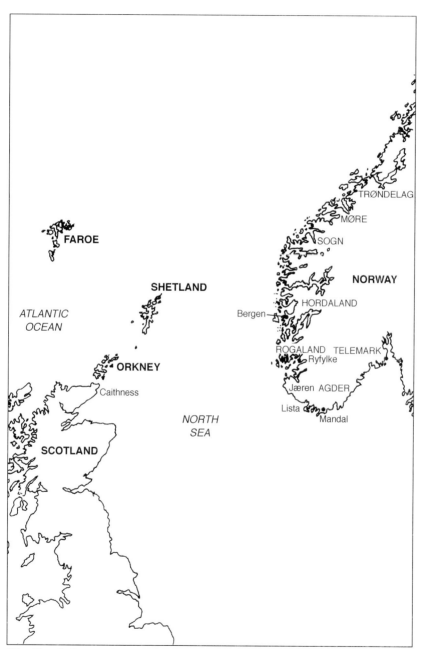

The North Sea and the North Atlantic.

NORN

'Norn' is a name that has been used to describe forms of Scandinavian speech current at one time in Orkney, Shetland and parts of Scotland. The language was brought across the North Sea by Viking invaders, and the word 'Norn' itself is derived from the Old Norse adjective *norrœnn* 'Norwegian, Norse' and the corresponding noun *norrœna* 'Norwegian language, Norse language'. In a broad sense Norn may thus designate Scandinavian as spoken in the Hebrides and on the Scottish Mainland as well as in Orkney and Shetland. However, because the language survived for so much longer in the Northern Isles, there has been a widespread tendency to apply Norn solely to the Orkney and Shetland situation — though some have also wanted to include north-eastern Caithness, an area intimately linked with the Norse Earldom of Orkney. Even in this narrower sense Norn is by no means an unambiguous term. To some it denotes any piece of Scandinavian language material emanating from the Northern Isles, including Viking-Age runic inscriptions[2] and medieval documents; to others it means only the spoken Scandinavian of the islands and written records of such speech. Norn may appear in yet other senses. Most confusingly, it is a name sometimes given to modern Shetland dialect (e.g. Sandison 1953). In the present work it is used to mean 'the distinctive form of Scandinavian speech that developed in the Northern Isles'.

A GENERAL OUTLINE OF THE HISTORY OF NORN

Although there was doubtless contact between Scandinavia and the Northern Isles before the Viking Age, there is nothing to suggest large-scale Scandinavian immigration before about 800. Even this date has to be treated with circumspection. Records are so meagre and often so difficult to interpret that some margin of error must be allowed for.

While it seems beyond dispute that the bulk of the settlers came from Norway, it is less easy to pinpoint the precise areas of that country from which they originated. Western rather than eastern Norway must have been the home of the majority, but 'western' in this context means anywhere from present-day Agder to Nord-Trøndelag.

The nature of the relations between the Scandinavian settlers and the indigenous population has been a matter of considerable controversy. It has been variously claimed that the Northern Isles were all but deserted before the Norsemen arrived, that the pre-Viking inhabitants were exterminated or driven out, or that they were assimilated. With the knowledge at our disposal today, gradual assimilation seems the most likely scenario. Whatever the true sequence of events, it is clear that the indigenous language or languages withered away, as a form of Scandinavian speech — presumably based chiefly on contemporary western Norwegian — became dominant.

This form of speech — the developing Norn — appears to have remained the chief, if not the sole, medium of communication in the islands for several centuries, but proximity to Scotland, where Scots — a northern form of English — was gaining ascendancy, led to a gradual weakening of its position. With the pledging of Orkney in 1468 and Shetland in 1469 to King James III of Scotland, not only the political but the linguistic fate of the Northern Isles was sealed: they were to become a fully integrated part of the Scottish and later the United Kingdom, and to adopt Scots and ultimately standard English (in writing at least) as their language(s).

Of the structure of Norn in the final centuries of its existence and of its relationship with Scots not a great deal is known. There is also considerable uncertainty and profound disagreement both about the date and the manner of Norn's demise. This is particularly true of the situation in Shetland, where speakers of the language are reported as late as the mid-nineteenth century. The reliability of such reports is, however, far from assured, and the bulk of the evidence tends to suggest that in both Orkney and Shetland Norn died out no later than the second half of the eighteenth century. In certain contexts it lives on. Most place-names in the Northern Isles are of Norse origin and there is a substantial, though declining, Scandinavian substratum in the dialects now spoken there.

THE HISTORY OF NORN IN DETAIL
1. THE ORIGIN OF NORN

First to be considered is the date of the Scandinavian settlement of the Northern Isles, the origin of the settlers, and the relationship of their language to that or those of the indigenous population.

There is surprisingly little direct evidence for the arrival of Scandinavian peoples in Orkney and Shetland. Literary sources tell of Viking raids in the British Isles towards the end of the eighth century, of the apparent settlement of a group of islands probably to be equated with the Faroes around 800 (Tierney 1967:74-7, 115-16), and of Norse emigration to Iceland c. 875. From this it has been deduced that Scandinavians are likely to have been arriving in Orkney and Shetland in considerable numbers by 800. Varying dates have been put on the earliest Norse archaeological remains (see the surveys in Wainwright 1962; Morris 1990), but all in all these do not appear to be in serious conflict with the literary testimony. Place-name evidence, especially the occurrence of the pre-Viking-Age generics -*heimr* 'home, dwelling' and -*vin* 'meadow, pasture', led at one time to the belief that an initial wave of colonisation must have taken place about the year 700 (cf., e.g., Jakobsen 1936:15-16), but modern scholarship tends to see the few -*heimr* and -*vin* formations that occur in the Northern Isles as stereotypes brought from Norway as ready-coined names (Fellows-Jensen 1984:153-4). More purely linguistic evidence of early settlement that has been offered concerns in particular the absence of the innovation known as *i*-mutation[3] in many Shetland Norn words. The emigrants, it is suggested, must have left their home country 'prior to the appearance of the i-mutation in Norse' (Jakobsen 1928-32:lx). Few, however, would now argue that *i*-mutation post-dates A.D. 700. Most would put it at 450-500 at the latest, and no one has seriously suggested that the settlers departed for Shetland in the fifth century or earlier. The wanting *i*-mutation must have a different explanation. Such evidence as there is thus seems in part to support and in no way to conflict with a settlement date of *c*. 800.

Regarding the place of origin of the settlers, the literary record strongly suggests a north-west Norwegian connection. *Orkneyinga saga*, the Icelandic account of the Orkney Earldom, probably composed largely in the late twelfth century, and *Heimskringla*, the Icelandic writer Snorri Sturluson's thirteenth-century history of the Norwegian kings, make an illegitimate son of Rǫgnvaldr Mœrajarl[4] the progenitor of the Earls of Orkney, while *Historia Norwegiæ*, a Latin history of Norway, perhaps from the end of the twelfth century, tells how relatives of the mighty Rogwald — assumed to be the same Earl Rǫgnvaldr — seized the Orkneys from their original inhabitants (Finnbogi Guðmundsson 1965:10-20; Bjarni Aðalbjarnarson 1941:128-9, 131-4; Storm 1880:89-90).[5] How much trust is to be placed in these accounts is another matter: all three claim that the events they describe took place in the reign of Haraldr hárfagri,[6] that is, about a hundred years after the probable Scandinavian settlement of the Northern Isles. Nevertheless, they may preserve traditions about a strong Møre presence among the ruling élite.

Archaeological evidence unfortunately offers little help in locating the settlers' homelands (cf., e.g., Wainwright 1962:143-4).

While the place-names of the Northern Isles seem to tie in most closely with those of Sogn, Møre and Trøndelag in north-western Norway (cf. Stewart 1987:22-4), it is worth remembering that the choice of particular names will depend to a considerable extent on local conditions. Not all have favoured a north-west Norwegian link. Jakobsen (1928-32:xxxiv-v) claims that onomastically it is 'the south-westerly and

3

southerly parts of Norway with which Shetland most fully agrees', and he also sees clear signs of south-east Norwegian naming practices. However, the only evidence he offers comes in the form of a general reference to 'more peculiar names'. Possibly it is the list of 'Ancient, rare Place-names in Norway recurring in Shetland' on pp.lxxvi-viii the reader is meant to consult for more specific guidance, but as a conclusive demonstration of the south-west and south (and perhaps also south-east) Norwegian origins of Shetland place-nomenclature it leaves something to be desired.

Jakobsen considered not only the place-names of Shetland (and Orkney), but also Norn vocabulary and phonology to point to south-west Norway as the area from which the bulk of the settlers came. It is undeniable that what we know of Norn, both the Orkney and Shetland variety, suggests a strong link with the Norwegian dialects of the south-west (those found in the area Vest-Agder to Sogn, Chapman 1962:114-20, referring to phonological features; 'Jæderen [modern Jæren] and Ryfylke', Marwick 1929:xlviii, also apparently referring chiefly to phonology; 'Bergen down to Lister and Mandal', Jakobsen 1928-32:xxxi, referring to vocabulary), but how far that reflects the immediate post-settlement situation rather than subsequent levelling we are unfortunately in no position to say. Jakobsen noted a certain amount of Danish input in Shetland Norn, some of which he regarded as ancient (1928-32:xxxiv), but although a few of the original settlers may indeed have hailed from Denmark (cf. the discussions in Wainwright 1962:142-3; Fellows-Jensen 1984:149), there is little doubt — Jakobsen's views notwithstanding — that such Danish as has been found in the Scandinavian of the Northern Isles stems from the period of Danish ascendancy over Norway (for an illustrative example, cf. Jakobsen 1928-32:cxvi-vii).

The safest, if most conservative, conclusion is that the vast majority of the settlers came from western Norway — from the area between present-day Nord-Trøndelag and Vest-Agder. There seems no warrant, however, for identifying one of these areas rather than another as the principal source of the emigration (on the 'south-west Norwegian' character of Norn, see further below).

Who inhabited Orkney and Shetland at the time of the Norse settlement and what happened to them have been the focus of considerable speculation. We learn little of either matter from medieval Scandinavian literary sources. Saga accounts ignore the indigenous population completely. *Historia Norwegiæ* tells of Norse subjugation of the *Peti* and *Papæ* of Orkney, the first a pygmy-like race of strange habits after whom the islands were called *terra Petorum* 'land of the *Peti*', the second a people who dressed in white cloaks like clerics, from which they got their name: 'unde in Theutonica lingua omnes clerici papæ dicuntur' 'all clerics in the Teutonic tongue being called *papæ*' (Storm 1880:88-9). The dearth of

4

information in the sagas has been put down to a complete lack of interest on the part of their authors. There may well be some truth in this, but it is still odd that not a single native leader, if only in the role of a straw opponent, puts in an appearance. That might perhaps be taken to indicate a lack of organised opposition to the Norse invaders, an interpretation the report in *Historia Norwegiæ* certainly does nothing to contradict.

Some scholars (e.g., Goudie 1904:xiv) have contended that the native population was well-nigh exterminated by the Norsemen, others (e.g., Brøgger 1930:257-66) that the islands had become virtually uninhabited before their arrival and that the settlement therefore proceeded peacefully. Neither of these extreme views corresponds with the archaeological and other evidence now at our disposal, which suggests at least a degree of co-existence (cf. Wainwright 1962:115-16; Morris 1990, especially 216-21; Ritchie 1990:200-01). Most recently Lamb (1993) has painted a picture of a highly-structured Carolingian-style Orkney, which the Norse settlers initially took over and administered as it was. The *Papæ* of *Historia Norwegiæ* in his interpretation are 'the pastoral hierarchy of the Roman Church' and the *Papa* place-names 'imply a recognition by the Norse, of estates held by the Church'. The Orkney Earldom, Lamb argues, represents a later stage 'when the Norse élite found that it no longer needed to rule through the old Pictish institutions' (p.268).

Whether or not one accepts Lamb's thesis, it seems certain that the *Papæ* were clerics of some sort, and not a race of people as they are mistakenly portrayed in *Historia Norwegiæ*. It is the *Peti* who appear to be the native population of Orkney, and it has been generally, and doubtless correctly, assumed that they are to be identified as Picts. Apart from anything else, the name *Peti*, like the first element of Norse *Péttlandsfjǫrðr* 'Pentland Firth', is surely related to Lat. *Picti* (Nicolaisen 1986:150-51).

This is not the place to go into the troublesome question of who the Picts were (cf. the discussion in Wainwright 1980). It will be enough to consider the conclusions of Jackson's thorough and careful examination of the language situation in Pictland (1980). Jackson is of the view that two languages were in use there, one a type of P-Celtic,[7] related, but probably not immediately, to the P-Celtic of Strathclyde, Wales and south-west England, the other a non-Indo-European language, presumably the speech of a people living in Britain before the coming of the Celts. The evidence adduced indicates that P-Celtic was the dominant language in southern Pictland, while in the north, including Orkney and Shetland, the non-Indo-European language appears to have been the one chiefly used.

Recently this view has been challenged, and the claim made that the language of Pictland was P-Celtic throughout (Forsyth forthcoming). It is argued that belief in the extended survival of a pre-Indo-European language in northern Britain owes much to the inscrutability of the evidence, in particular the Pictish ogam[8] inscriptions, and conflicts with general experience of language shift and language death. That a personal or place-name cannot easily be shown to be Celtic or an inscription immediately understood does not in itself, Forsyth argues, demonstrate the existence of an otherwise unknown tongue.

This is ultimately a question for scholars of Celtic to resolve. Whether the inhabitants of Orkney and Shetland spoke one or two languages at the time the Norsemen arrived, and what language or languages these were, does not impinge greatly on the establishment of Scandinavian in the islands since, as will be emphasised in the following, indigenous speech appears to have exerted no influence at all on the developing Norn. One piece of evidence is worth quoting, however. The *Ravenna Cosmography*, written about a hundred years before the beginning of the Norse settlement, observes that different groups of people had different names for the same Orkney islands (Rivet and Smith 1979:215). While in no way offering proof of the survival of a pre-Indo-European language, this little snippet of information seems to fit better Jackson's conception of the linguistic situation in the north of Pictland than Forsyth's.

It has been claimed that a further language must also have existed in the Northern Isles before the coming of the Norsemen. The presence of ogam inscriptions and the likelihood of Irish-Scottish participation in the Christianisation of northern Pictland suggest at least knowledge of and perhaps limited use of Q-Celtic.[7] Jakobsen (1936:175-207) also thought he recognised a number of pre-Norse place-names of Q-Celtic origin, but, to the extent that they are Q-Celtic at all, most of these are now regarded as of post-settlement origin — names adopted by Norse settlers in the Gaelic-speaking regions to the south and west and brought from there to Orkney and Shetland (Fellows-Jensen 1984:152). The *Papæ* of *Historia Norwegiæ* and the many place-names containing the element *pap-* in the Northern Isles have been taken as evidence of the presence of Irish religious hermits, but as Lamb points out (1993:266-7), the equation does not work. Since many of the *pap-* names were given not to remote and isolated sites but to prime-quality farmland, they can only have designated church estates. While it is thus possible that these places were the home of Q-Celtic-speaking clerics, they are just as likely to have been inhabited by Pictish churchmen speaking a non-Indo-European language and/or P-Celtic (certainly the latter since many would have come from the Pictish heartlands to the south). The evidence for the existence of pre-settlement Q-Celtic in Orkney and Shetland must, on this showing, be deemed tenuous. There are the ogam inscriptions, but although they exhibit the two formulaic words MEQQ and CRROSCC, presumably derived from the Gaelic words for 'son' and 'cross' (if the latter does not come more immediately from Latin), these writings have

6

for the most part proved indecipherable; possibly, as Jackson maintained, they are manifestations of a pre-Celtic non-Indo-European tongue — the 'other language' of Pictland. Finally in this connection it is worth noting that the *Vita s. Findani* 'Life of St Findan', probably written in the late ninth century by an Irishman resident on the Continent (Holder-Egger 1887; Thomson and Omand 1986), implicitly contrasts knowledge of Irish as a foreign language among some Orcadian churchmen with total ignorance of it among the population at large, who in the 840s — the time of St Findan's sojourn in Orkney — can hardly yet have been Norse speaking, but must still have used the indigenous tongue or tongues.

The Scandinavians who arrived to settle the Northern Isles *c.* 800 may, then, have been confronted with one, two or possibly three unfamiliar languages. What happened in the contact situation that ensued is hard to reconstruct because of lack of evidence. The outcome was the complete dominance of Scandinavian and the disappearance of the other languages, but the manner of the transition and the timescale involved are matters about which we can for the most part only speculate. Seen in general terms, the advance of Scandinavian in Orkney and Shetland looks not unlike that of Anglo-Saxon in England: a complete linguistic conquest, in which virtually all traces of earlier speech, including place and personal names, are wiped out. This seems to indicate swift subjugation rather than the co-existence and gradual take-over envisaged by Lamb. It is, however, unclear how far the Anglo-Saxon analogy can be pressed. There is really nothing in the linguistic evidence to conflict with the view that the incoming Scandinavians reached some kind of accommodation with the native population to start with, only to take over positions of power and authority as the settlement built up. If, as Lamb suggests (1993:268), there is a connection between the establishment of the Orkney Earldom and a delayed assumption of total power by the Scandinavians, the final collapse of Pictish authority in the Northern Isles will presumably have come towards the end of the ninth century. This would still have given the settlers several hundred years of undisputed control — time enough to impose their Scandinavian language and culture on the conquered territory to the almost total exclusion of what had existed before.

A small piece of evidence that is said to 'point to a very mixed language in Shetland in the late ninth or early tenth century' (Jackson 1980:142) is the Bressay inscription. This reads, transliterated from ogam (the dividers are placed in accordance with the drawing in Macalister 1940:199):

CRROSCC:NAHHTVVDDADDS:DATTRR:ANN
BENNIS:ESMEQQDDRROA:NN

Here we have not only CRROSCC and MEQQ, the words of Gaelic or probable Gaelic origin referred to above, but supposedly also Norse

7

DATTRR 'daughter' — side by side with elements of what appears to be an unknown language. The use of dots as dividers, possibly adopted from Norse runic practice, and the doubling of consonants, found in Irish ogam inscriptions, are offered as further evidence of linguistic mix. The occurrence of Gaelic elements in Pictish ogams seems assured, though whether these ever amounted to more than a few formulaic expressions and the odd epigraphic practice, both perhaps taken over with the alphabet itself, is uncertain. To the extent that DATTRR *is* Norse (it might after all be a Pictish word or element, given that so little of the inscription otherwise is comprehensible), and the use of two dots as a division mark *is* borrowed from runic writing, we may have evidence of Scandinavian influence on the (or an) indigenous language of Shetland (and by extrapolation Orkney); on the other hand, these features may show nothing more than that the Picts adopted formulaic elements and epigraphic practices from the Scandinavians as well as the Irish. The clearest inference to be drawn from the Bressay stone (and, to the extent they are of a similar date, from other Pictish ogams of Orkney and Shetland) is that an indigenous language continued to be sufficiently in favour to be used in a formal inscription a hundred years or more after the Scandinavian settlement.

Scandinavian and Pictish (however this is understood) thus seem to have lived side by side for a century at

Pictured right: The Bressay Stone.
Photo: National Museums of Scotland

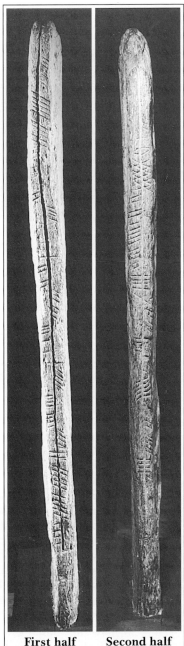

First half   **Second half**

least. Perhaps the co-existence persisted a while longer, but by the late twelfth century when *Historia Norwegiæ* was (in all probability) composed, the native people of Orkney appear to have become a distant memory — though it is worth bearing in mind that the author's view of the *Peti* as a race of dwarfs with supernatural attributes may have been based on a source remote from the Northern Isles.

Scandinavian and Gaelic obviously co-existed in many parts of Scotland as well as in Ireland, and various kinds of Gaelic influence on the Scandinavian of the British Isles has been noted. Very little, if any, of this influence seems to be specific to Orkney and Shetland, however, even though the Orkney Earldom is sometimes portrayed as a cultural frontier zone — a centre for the transmission of Irish-Scottish beliefs and traditions to the wider Scandinavian world (cf., e.g., Crawford 1987:211-13). While it would be unwise to deny totally the presence of Gaelic speakers in Orkney and Shetland — either before the arrival of the Norsemen or subsequently — it is unlikely that the status or numbers of such as there were ever enabled them to exert an influence on the developing form of Scandinavian in the islands. The traces of Gaelic that we find in medieval Norse writings with a Northern-Isles connection, in Orkney and Shetland place-names, and in Norn, seem to be part of the general currency of Scandinavian North-Atlantic parlance.

In the light of what has been said, it is not surprising to learn that there is no observable substratum in Norn — neither Celtic nor non-Celtic. As we shall see, our knowledge of Norn is too sketchy for us to be completely confident no such substratum existed, but it must seem unlikely. Scandinavian culture and language appear to have become totally dominant by the middle of the eleventh century, if not before, and the wholesale replacement of pre-Norse place-names suggests either lack of communication between settlers and natives — perhaps unlikely in view of the various points made above — or a low regard by the incomers for the language or languages of the people they displaced.

2. THE DEVELOPMENT OF NORN

The establishment of a form of Scandinavian as the principal and ultimately the sole language of Orkney and Shetland did not signify a change from a non-literary to a literary culture. The Picts, as we have seen, had developed a rudimentary epigraphic tradition, and the *Papæ* clearly belonged to the world of medieval European learning (whatever their status, there can be no doubt that they were churchmen of some sort, and *Historia Norwegiæ* — otherwise silent on their fate — reports that they left books behind). The Scandinavian incomers for their part do not appear to have set much store by writing, either in runes or in the roman alphabet. Even allowing that a fair amount has perished (see below), the written record of the period of Scandinavian ascendancy in the Northern Isles can only be described as pitiful. With the adoption of Christianity by the Norsemen there must clearly have been a segment of the population that was literate, and in the twelfth century the Orkney earl, Rǫgnvaldr Kali, and his circle seem to have provided a focus for high secular culture, which doubtless included writing, but in terms of schools, scriptoria and literary tradition the situation in the Northern Isles resembles that in Faroe rather than Norway or Iceland: signs of activity are few and far between.

The consequence is a scarcity of documentary evidence on which to base a description of Orkney and Shetland Scandinavian and its development. The available source material can be divided into six categories: (1) runic inscriptions; (2) documents written in the roman alphabet; (3) continuous pieces of spoken Norn recorded before the language died; (4) words and forms preserved in Scaldic verse;[9] (5) place-names; (6) fragments of spoken Norn recorded before and relics recorded after the language died. On the face of it this seems a sizeable corpus, and indeed for those interested in vocabulary there is much to be learnt. It is, however, only the runic inscriptions, the documents and the lengthier pieces of spoken Norn that might be expected to yield information about the language in function, and as source material all three suffer from one or more drawbacks. Any account of the development of Norn must nevertheless clearly start with an examination of these three sources: their quality needs to be assessed and the information that can be gleaned from them summarised. A brief analysis of each therefore follows. The picture of Northern-Isles Scandinavian that emerges will then be compared with the residual material: forms in Scaldic verse, place-names, and the fragments of Norn, including individual lexical items, collected between the sixteenth and twentieth centuries.

Runic inscriptions

At the latest count Orkney can boast fifty-two inscriptions considered by scholars to be runic and of likely Viking-Age or medieval origin. Shetland is less well endowed, having but seven (for texts and discussion of the Orkney and Shetland inscriptions, cf. Barnes 1993; 1994; six have been added since the 1993 account). The Orkney total is boosted by the thirty-three carvings found in Maeshowe, the famous pre-historic chambered cairn in Stenness. However, as the present author has argued in another connection (Barnes 1991a), it cannot be shown conclusively that any of the Maeshowe inscriptions were made by native islanders, and the probability is that the majority were carved by visiting Norwegians. Indeed, the glaring contrast between the versatility exhibited in Maeshowe and the sorry collection of runic odds and ends from elsewhere in Orkney is itself an indication of imported skill.

10

Few of the Shetland or Orkney inscriptions (save those in Maeshowe, cf. p.35) can be satisfactorily dated: of many all one can say with reasonable certainty is that they are pre-Reformation — provided, of course, none is a modern imitation (for some discussion of this question, see Barnes 1993:37-9). Interpretation is often a serious problem: while almost everything in Maeshowe makes tolerable sense, only some nine or ten of the twenty-six other inscriptions from the Northern Isles have so far yielded anything approaching a comprehensible text, and in six of these cases the text is fragmentary. Maeshowe excluded, the corpus provides few pointers to the linguistic background of the writers: the language — what little there is of it — cannot be distinguished from that of contemporary Norwegian inscriptions. This confirms the west Scandinavian character of the developing Norn, but nothing further.

Documents in the roman alphabet

Here we are faced at the outset with the problem of delimiting the corpus. Which Scandinavian-language documents should be included? Any, it might initially be thought, that exhibit characteristically Norn features. But this is clearly unworkable. Apart from anything else, we do not know all the features we should be looking for, and even if we did, their absence might be as revealing as their presence. Two possible approaches suggest themselves: the net can be cast wide to take in all documents with an Orkney or Shetland connection, or the selection can be limited to those written in the Northern Isles. The first procedure assures comprehensive coverage, but is more suited to an in-depth study. The second is therefore the one adopted here. Problems remain, however. They concern in particular the provenance of certain documents, and the fact that even where an Orkney or Shetland location can be established as the place of origin, there is seldom an indication of the scribe's identity and certainly none of where he learnt to write. Almost any Scandinavian-language document emanating from the Northern Isles could in theory have been written by a Norwegian or by someone who had received his scribal training in Norway (in some cases a Swedish or Danish background is also possible). Scribal training in the motherland is in fact highly probable: there is no evidence of schools in Shetland prior to c. 1611 and in Orkney only the Kirkwall Grammar School seems to go back to the medieval period.

The following are the Scandinavian-language documents which either give an Orkney or Shetland locality as their place of origin or whose Northern-Isles provenance can be inferred from the contents (published in DN unless otherwise stated, and identified by their DN number): from Orkney — II 168 (1329), II 170 (1329), I 404 (1369), II 691 (c. 1425); from Shetland — I 89 (1299), I 109 (1307), I 340 (1355), III 284 (1355), III 310 (1360), II 797 (1452), II 859 (1465), VI 651 (1509), Goudie

1904:81-2 (1545), unpublished copy of 1431 document from Kaldbak (c. 1550), OSR 74 (1586). Further documents have been drawn into the discussion, the majority chiefly because they were included by Goudie in his 1904 work (78-131). Goudie's chief concern, however, was to show that Scandinavian continued to be used by Shetland officials long after the impignoration in 1469, and most of the material he prints was actually written in Norway (a circumstance he by and large acknowledges but which has sometimes been overlooked by others, cf. Smith 1990:29). Only one of Goudie's documents is definitely of Shetland provenance (that of 1545, cf. above); two others, dated 1602 and 1607, he assumes to have been written in the islands (1904:109-10), but as Brian Smith has pointed out (personal communication to the author): 'I see no evidence that the receipts of 1602 and 1607 were written, as opposed to being *signed*, in Shetland.' He argues that they could well have been written by an agent for a Norwegian landowner, to be taken to Shetland, and emphasises that the 1607 receipt — widely hailed as the last Scandinavian-language document from the islands (e.g. Geipel 1971:90-91; Grønneberg 1981:3; Barnes 1984:354) — is 'signed by a Shetlander with a mark — i.e. he didn't (/couldn't) write it'. This latter point is uncertain. Goudie's printed version (1904:109-10) suggests that the granter of the 1607 document, Vellem Monsøn (Uisted?), signed with his own hand; the mark may have been included as additional confirmation. The un-Scandinavian appearance of the phrase <an half can smor> in the 1602 receipt should also be noted. Both originals now seem to be lost, however, so in neither case can the reading be checked. Also worth mentioning is OSR 35 (1491), written at <Borgh>. Smith (again, personal communication) urges caution in assuming that this was a *Borg* in Shetland and denies the claim by the editors of OSR that it was Sumburgh; in his view the letter is as likely to have been written in Norway as in Shetland.

This is in truth not a very impressive testimony of epistolary activity. No doubt a goodly number of documents have perished (cf. Marwick 1929:xxi-ii on indications of substantial loss in Orkney; Ballantyne and Smith 1994:xix-xx *re* Shetland), but the contrast with Norway is striking — and indeed with the other countries (bar Faroe) in which a form of Scandinavian continued to be the language generally used. It is not as though Orkney and Shetland were societies largely without need of documentary witness: as administrators, officials and others begin to write in Scots in the fifteenth and sixteenth centuries, the volume of paperwork can be seen to increase rapidly. One is led to wonder — there being little in the way of firm evidence — how widespread literacy in Scandinavian can have been in the Northern Isles.

Divergent views have been expressed on the linguistic significance of the Scandinavian-language documents written in Orkney and Shetland.

12

Marwick (1929:xxi) reports his 'complete failure to find any...'Orkneyisms'" in the four Orcadian examples, while Indrebø (1951:281) considered that 'fornbrevi frå Hjaltland og Orknøyane syner at mange av dei viktugaste serdragi i målet på øyane ovra seg alt i millomnorsk tid' ('the diplomas from Shetland and Orkney indicate that many of the most important characteristics of the language of the islands appeared as early as the Middle Norwegian period'). Recent investigations by the author have revealed only a few sporadic features in the fifteen documents that might distinguish them from similar contemporary writings in Norway. There is of course, as noted above, the problem of knowing what one is looking for. Points of comparison — in addition to Old West Scandinavian — can only be spoken Norn (first cited in the sixteenth century), and Icelandic, Faroese, and western Norwegian dialects. Northern-Isles Scandinavian may *a priori* be surmised to have developed along similar lines to these latter three, though such a hypothesis seems to require confidence either in the possibility of long-range influence or in the murky concept of linguistic drift[10] — or perhaps a combination of both. Taking these points of comparison and applying them to the documents concerned, one comes up with the following.

(1)   <i> for /e/ in demonstratives: <þitta> for *þetta* 'this', <þis> for *þess* 'that' (Orkn. 1369) (cf. Marwick 1929:xl; Hægstad 1900:47).

(2)   Traces of <u> for /o:/ and /o/: (e.g.) <landbular> for *landbólar* 'tenants' (Orkn. 1369), <w> for *ór* (also *úr*) 'out of' (Orkn. *c*. 1425), <brut> for *brot* 'transgressions' (Orkn. 1369), <opburit> for *uppborit* 'received' (Orkn. *c*. 1425) (cf. Marwick 1929:xli; Hægstad 1900:37-8).

(3)   Traces of monophthongisation of /au/: <ustan> for *austan* 'from the east' (Shetl. 1299), <buð> for *bauð* 'offered' (Shetl. 1307), <sode> for *sauði* 'sheep' (Shetl. *c*. 1550) (cf. Hægstad 1900:43-5; Jakobsen 1928-32:l).

(4)   Apparent unrounding of vowels: (e.g.) <frista> for *fyrsta* 'first', <nita> for *nýta* 'enjoy', <beta> for *bœta* 'pay', <tolfuo ret> for *tólfrœtt* 'consisting of twelve tens' (Orkn. 1369) (cf. Marwick 1929:xlii; Hægstad 1900:40-41).

(5)   <g> for /k/: <luga> for *lúka* 'pay' (Orkn. 1369) (cf. Marwick 1929:xlvii; Hægstad 1900:64-8).

(6)   Confusion of <m> and <n> in final position: <son> for *som* 'who' (Orkn. *c*. 1425), <skyldem> for *skyldin* 'debt, rent', <thenn> for *þeim* 'them' (Shetl. 1586) (cf. Hægstad 1900:65).

(7)   Confusion of <h> and <þ>: <i þia> for *í hjá* 'present' (Shetl. 1355 — DN III 284) (cf. Hægstad 1900:68; Marwick 1929:xlvii).

(8)   Absence of initial <h>: <æita> for *heita* 'are called' (Orkn. 1369) (cf. Marwick 1929:xlv, xlvii; Hægstad 1900:63; Jakobsen 1928-32:liv).

13

(9)   Instances of Scots influence — (i) on syntax: <insigle aff theris egitt> 'seals of their own' (Shetl. 1586); — (ii) on vocabulary: (e.g.) <cont> 'count, reckoning', <minister> (Shetl. 1586); — (iii) on orthography and/or word forms: <guidir> 'good' (nom. m. sg.) (Shetl. *c.* 1550), <godman> (Scots *guidman* rather than Scand. *god man* 'solid citizen'?) (Orkn. *c.* 1425).

Further to point (9), we find the scribe of Orkn. 1369 providing examples of apocope and metathesis,[11] and demonstrating woeful ignorance of the Old West Scandinavian inflexional system. More than one document employs *hans* 'his' with reflexive function in place of the reflexive possessive *sinn* 'his own' (though this could be a medieval Danish usage rather than the result of interference from Scots *his*, cf. Falk and Torp 1900:134-5). It also seems likely that the <quh-> in <quharium> (i.e. ON *hverjum* 'each, every', Shetl. *c.* 1550) is the traditional Scots written form of earlier English [hw-] rather than a reflection of the common West Scandinavian sound change [hw-] > [kv-].

It is not immediately obvious what conclusions are to be drawn from the above list. Some of the features noted can be found in Norwegian — or in Swedish and Danish, both of which influenced Norwegian in the late Middle Ages — but there are reasons for thinking they may equally well be Northern-Isles Scandinavian. The use of <i> for /e/ in demonstratives can be paralleled in medieval Danish and Swedish, but the examples are very few and far between. The occurrence of <u> where Old West Norse has /o/ is a general East Scandinavian phenomenon, but coupled with <u> for /o:/, and in the light of certain Scaldic forms (see below) and the regular representation of historical /o/, /o:/ by <u> in records of spoken Norn (Hægstad 1900:37-8; Marwick 1929:xli), such spellings may be accorded significance (cf., however, the counter-example <ondher> for *undir* 'under, to' (Shetl. 1465 — unless it is a reverse spelling[12]), and the view espoused by Pettersen (1988) that Orkn. *c.* 1425 is linguistically Swedish). Monophthongisation of the falling diphthongs /ei/ > /e:/, /au/, /øy/ > /ø:/ is a Danish, Swedish and East Norwegian as well as a Northern-Isles phenomenon, and to that extent <redum> for *reiðum* 'ready' (Shetl. 1355 — DN I 340), although early, may reflect East Scandinavian influence, but <u> and <o> for /au/ are more reminiscent of the Norn forms we find later. The unrounding of certain vowels, or of vowels in particular environments, are common enough phenomena in the Scandinavian dialects, but the large number of examples of <i> for /y/ and <e> for /ø:/ in Orkn. 1369 (apparently documenting a general difficulty with front rounded vowels) looks unusual and might be due to Scots influence (though /ø/ in fact survives in the Scots dialects of Orkney and Shetland). Danish influence ensures that the appearance of <b>, <d>, <g> for /p/, /t/, /k/ becomes a regular feature of Norwegian writing in the fifteenth century, but 1369 is very early for this, and <luga> for *lúka* 'pay' may thus reflect the parallel weakening or voicing that took place in Norn. The change: final unstressed /-m/ > /-n/ is documented extensively in one Shetland Norn text (the *Hildina* ballad, see p.17 below) and sporadically in others, the most frequent example being <sin> (<sen>, <san>) for the relative particle *sem, som*. Norwegian is no stranger to the spelling <þj> for /hj/ (cf. Indrebø 1951:234), where, judging by modern dialect forms, it indicates the coalescence of /hj/ with affricates or developing palatal spirants;[13] <i þia> for *í hjá* (Shetl. 1355 — DN III 284) may thus be a Norwegian form, but it could also reflect Norn pronunciation, given that Faroese undergoes a similar development — if it is not to be seen as a reverse spelling following the sporadic change /þ/ > /h/ (see below). Loss of initial /h-/ is not unknown in medieval Norwegian either (cf. Seip 1955:162, 276), but it is particularly prevalent in Shetland Norn. Direct influence from Scots seems largely restricted to vocabulary items reflecting innovations in the islands, but the 1586 syntactic borrowing <aff theris egitt> may be symptomatic of more extensive linguistic interference.

Some of the above forms might be dismissed as spelling mistakes. It is, for example, easy to imagine a scribe writing <ustan> for *austan* or <son> for *som*. But these are not isolated occurrences: they find support both in related contemporary spellings and in later Norn. The initial presumption must therefore be that they are intentional. There are other apparently non-Norwegian (and non-Swedish/Danish) forms in the fifteen documents, which are harder to tie in with any pattern: these are perhaps more likely to be scribal blunders or idiosyncrasies, but there is always a chance they too may reflect the spoken language of the Northern Isles. A recurring feature in Orkn. 1369 is the omission of <l> immediately before certain consonants (<skide> for *skyldi* 'should, was to', <Hiatlanð> for *Hjaltland* 'Shetland' (possibly through contamination with *Hetland*?), and cf. the apparent reverse spelling <halfua> for *hafa* 'have'), but loss of /l/ in this particular set of environments does not seem to characterise any known form of Scandinavian (we find that /l/ is lost before /v/ in the modern Norwegian dialects of Telemark and Sætesdal, for example, but retained before /d/ and /t/ — cf. Aasen 1848:56).

It is noteworthy that some of the more striking features of (at least certain kinds of) spoken Norn (e.g. /rn/, /n:/ > /dn/, intercalation of /g/ between vowels) do not make an appearance in the medieval documents that have been considered here. This, as well as the fact that such suggestive features as can be found occur only very infrequently, indicates that those who wrote in Scandinavian in Orkney and Shetland tended to follow the patterns of a well-established written tradition.

Indeed, if we are to trust the scanty records of spoken Norn that have come down to us, there must have been an ever-widening gulf between what users of Scandinavian said and wrote in the Northern Isles. The documents by and large reflect the changing written idiom of Norway; the fifteenth and sixteenth-century material, for example, implies a gradual Danicising of the language and a complete breakdown of the Old Norse inflexional system. Everyday speech in Orkney and Shetland, on the other hand, appears to have developed in much the same way as Faroese and, to a lesser extent, the more conservative dialects of western Norway: only limited Danicisation is evident, while the essentials of the inflexional system seem still to have been intact in the sixteenth century, and in Shetland at least to have remained so in the seventeenth and possibly even into the eighteenth. This dichotomy between speech and writing may have come about because, as has been suggested, many or most of the documents emanating from the Northern Isles were the work of Norwegian scribes or scribes trained in Norway. But even if they were in fact penned by natives trained in the islands, it is hard to see what traditions of writing they could have been trained in other than those of Norway.

Spoken Norn

For knowledge of the spoken Scandinavian of Orkney and Shetland we rely chiefly on material collected or published in the eighteenth century, by which time the language or languages (see below) may have been in the last stages of decline. The principal sources are: an Orkney Lord's Prayer published in Wallace 1700 (no manuscript exists and the printed version therefore has the status of primary evidence); a Shetland Lord's Prayer, a thirty-five stanza ballad and a list of thirty words collected by George Low in Foula in 1774 and extant in the manuscript of his *A Tour through the Islands of Orkney and Schetland* (cf. Low 1879:104-14). Beyond this there exist only a few isolated snatches of Norn from the period when it can be supposed still to have been a living language.[14]

I have described elsewhere (1984:356-62) the salient features of Orkney and Shetland Norn as they appear in the above records, and a linguistic commentary (dealing chiefly with morphology) accompanies the pieces printed on pp.44-6, 48. More detailed if somewhat antiquated accounts of this form (or these forms) of Scandinavian can be found in Marwick 1929 (xxix-xlviii) and Hægstad 1900 (cf. also more recently Rendboe 1987:81-96; 1990:62-85). It will be enough here to rehearse a few conclusions.

The phonological system of Norn seems to have moved quite a long way from its Old West Scandinavian origins — if we are right in believing there once existed a unified West Scandinavian system similar to that of twelfth-century Icelandic (as described in the contemporary *First*

Grammatical Treatise, cf. Hreinn Benediktsson 1972). In particular we may note that Norn shares a number of retentions and innovations with dialects of south-west Norway — first and foremost the following: (i) the preservation of unstressed /a/; (ii) /p/, /t/, /k/ > /b/, /d/, /g/ in intervocalic and final postvocalic position; (iii) /rn/ > /dn/; (iv) /n:/ > /dn/; (v) /l:/ > /dl/ (contrast, however, /fn/ > /mn/, a north-west and east Norwegian feature; the Scandinavian-language documents from the Northern Isles tend to have <fn> except where a further consonant follows the cluster, triggering the widespread change /fn/ > /m/, e.g., <jamgoðar> 'equally good, of equal value' (Shetl. 1307), <fornemdhan> 'aforesaid' (Shetl. 1465)). Even more striking are the parallels with Faroese: in addition to the five features already mentioned, which occur in all or some dialects of this language, we find in particular the following: (i) the intercalation of /g/ (Faroese /gv/), e.g., ON *sjór* > Far. *sjógvur*, Norn <sheug> 'sea'; (ii) /m/ > /n/ in weakly stressed final position, e.g., ON *honum* > Far. *honum* /honun/, Norn <honon> 'him [dat.]'; (iii) /þ/ > /h/ in some demonstratives and adverbs, e.g., ON *þetta* > Far. *hetta*, Norn <ita> (< **hitta*) 'this'. A possible further parallel concerns the diphthongisation product of ON /a:/, cf. Far. *á* /ɔa/, Norn <wo> 'on', but contrast <ro> 'advice', <fro> 'from' (Faroese /rɔa/, /frɔa/), where no diphthongisation is indicated in Norn (see further p.20 below).

The morphological and syntactic system of Norn too has undergone changes, many of which also characterise Faroese. Considerable simplification of the verbal paradigms has taken place; personal inflection seems largely to have disappeared, and to have been replaced in some verb types and tenses by a singular-plural distinction (based mainly on the third person forms) and in others (as far as can be judged) by a single ending. There are also sporadic indications of a breakdown in the case system of nouns and adjectives, but here the Old Norse pattern for the most part still prevails (cf., however, below on late Orkney Norn). The personal pronouns too have suffered changes. For Old West Scandinavian *ek* 'I' we find *yach*, *yagh* and *a*, for *vér* 'we' (or *vit* 'we two') *vi*, and for *þér* 'you [pl.]' (or *þit* 'you two') *di*. These forms could all be native developments, but *yach*, *yagh* and *vi* could also be due to the influence of Swedish and Danish, evident in the Scandinavian-language documents emanating from Orkney and Shetland from the fifteenth century onwards. The use of the (originally) dative form *dem* (Old West Scandinavian *þeim* 'them') for the accusative is paralleled in numerous forms of Scandinavian, but might conceivably be due to influence from Scots *them*. As a purely syntactic point it is worth noting that Norn, like Faroese and Icelandic, but unlike post-Reformation Danish, Swedish and Norwegian, exhibits subjectless sentences, e.g. *gede min vara to din* 'spoken will be of you' (rather than 'it [subj.] will be spoken of you' — i.e. 'you will be famous').

17

Norn vocabulary shows signs of Scots influence, but only on a fairly superficial level. This points to a situation similar to the one reflected in the Shetland document from 1586.

The picture of Norn as it emerges from this discussion should not be accepted without reservation. For one thing, the texts — primarily a traditional ballad and the Lord's Prayer — are unlikely to be representative of contemporary usage. For another, three of the items — including the only continuous piece of any length — were collected by one man, who clearly knew no form of Scandinavian, from one small, isolated island on one occasion. What is described above as 'Norn' is thus in reality almost entirely late eighteenth-century Foula Norn as heard and written down by someone who did not understand it. Nor do the problems end there. Although William Henry, the informant who provided Low with the ballad, is said to have been the descendant of a long line of Foula people (Baldwin 1984:59), it is important to note (a) that Foula was devastated by plague (presumably small-pox) in 1720 and repopulated from other parts of Shetland (Edmondston 1809:85; Baldwin 1984:55, who proposes an earlier epidemic around 1700) and (b) that there are several traditions of Faroese fishermen being cast ashore at 'Dale of Walls' and subsequently settling on the West Side and in Foula (Baldwin 1984:50; Shetland Archives D.1/172/28/2-3). It is of course highly improbable that the arrival of the odd Faroeman would be sufficient to cause Faroese features to spread among the speakers even of a small island community using a closely related language. Nevertheless these glimpses of Foula's past underline the dangers of misinterpretation that lurk in so small and unrepresentative a body of evidence.

The Orkney Lord's Prayer is unfortunately too brief to provide much of a corrective to the Foula material. Even so, points of contrast can be found. Orkney <fro olt ilt>, for example, as opposed to Foula <fro adlu idlu [dat. n.]> 'from all evil', suggests earlier abandonment of case distinctions in some Norn-speaking areas than others, while being tantalizingly non-committal about the development of ON /l:/ outside Foula (it is unclear precisely what sounds the <lt> spellings denote, but /l:/ > /dl/ immediately before a consonant would be unexpected in any form of Scandinavian). If there exists more solid counter-evidence to what the chance of preservation has left us, it can only be in the residual material — the Scaldic forms, the place-names, and the various fragments of Norn.

Residual sources

Such Scaldic verse as we have that was or may have been composed by Orkneymen is preserved in Icelandic manuscripts. Nevertheless, there are suggestions that the poems *Krákumál* 'The lay of Kráka' (twelfth century), *Jómsvíkingadrápa* 'The lay of the Jómsvikings' and the so-called *Málsháttakvæði* 'The proverb poem' (both the latter late twelfth or early thirteenth century and attributed to the Orkney bishop, Bjarni Kolbeinsson) contain specifically Orcadian words and probable Orcadian or 'Island' forms (Marwick 1929:xviii-xix; Olsen 1932:147-53).[15] There is little here, however, that can help determine the shape or structure of Norn. Forms such as <mvla> for *mola* 'crumb' and <fva> for *fóa* 'fox' suggest that the use of <u> for historical /o/, /o:/ in certain diplomas may have a basis in early sound changes, and there is slight evidence for one or two other pre-thirteenth-century alterations in the vowel system, but that is really all. The Scaldic verse is too close to the settlement period and preserved too far from Orkney for there to be a realistic hope it could throw much light on the development of Northern-Isles Scandinavian.

Place-names can offer but limited insight into the structure of a language, but are the carriers of considerable amounts of phonological and lexical information. The lexical significance of Orkney and Shetland place-nomenclature with regard to the geographical origins of the Norse settlers has been touched on earlier. Phonologically the place-names tend to duplicate the evidence of other sources, but occasionally they provide striking confirmation of what these sources only suggest. Perhaps the most telling example concerns /þ/ > /h/. We have seen possible indications of the change in a 1355 Shetland diploma, and somewhat firmer evidence in Low's 1774 Foula material. The occurrence of several Orkney place-names with original first element *Þór-*, late sixteenth-century <Hur->, <Hor->, now <Hur->, <Hour-> '[the god] Þórr', shows not only that our interpretation of Foula forms such as <ita> as derived from *þetta* via *hitta* is likely to be right, but that the change may well have occurred late in the life of Norn, was certainly widespread, and affected much the same words as in Faroese (certain pronouns and adverbs, and the god-name *Þórr*).

Fragments of Norn come from as early as the sixteenth century. The oldest, the Orkney greeting <goand da boundæ> recorded by 'Jo Ben' and glossed by him 'Guid day Guidman' (Marwick 1929:xxiv, 224), seems to show that Orcadian Norn preserved at least parts of the case system at this time (<goand da> is acc. m. sg., just as the corresponding *góðan dag* in Faroese and Icelandic), whereas in the approximately 150-year younger Orkney Lord's Prayer nominative, accusative and dative appear to have coalesced (see above and pp.48-9). From the late seventeenth century we have the Shetlandic terms <Yealtaland> 'Shetland', <Yalts> 'Shetlanders' and <Yaltmol> 'Shetland language' (Sibbald 1845:11, 68), which indicate an absence of progressive *i*-mutation[16] just as, for example, <Iarlin> 'the earl', <yamna> 'always' in the *Hildina* ballad. To the extent that Norn paralleled west rather than east

19

Norwegian patterns of speech, we would not expect progressive *i*-mutation to have taken place, but it is worth noting that the modern word *sheltie*, supposedly derived from *hjalti* 'Shetlander' but now used chiefly to denote 'Shetland pony', has root vowel [ɛ].

The bulk of Norn fragments are from the period when the language was no longer spoken. The best known and most prolific collectors of the dying embers of Scandinavian in the Northern Isles were the Faroeman Jakob Jakobsen (cf. Grønneberg 1981; Barnes 1996), active in the 1890s, and the Orcadian Hugh Marwick (cf. Dickins 1966-9), who worked in the early decades of the present century. The nature of the material amassed by these two scholars — words in the main — means that it is more suited to a study of late Norn vocabulary and phonology than morphology and syntax, and even in the case of phonology one comes up against a number of intractable problems (cf. Barnes 1991b:433-9).

The vocabulary, as was shown above, has been used in attempts to locate the area from which the settlers originated and as a means of measuring the closeness of Norn's kinship to other forms of Scandinavian. It can probably also tell us something about the language in its dying stages: the substantial lexical substratum bequeathed to Orkney and Shetland Scots seems to reflect a period in which Norn was used chiefly in the context of fishing, farming and the home. There are also considerable differences between the Norn lexica of Orkney and Shetland as they appear in Jakobsen 1928-32 and Marwick 1929. This is most plausibly explained partly as a result of the earlier and more radical Scotticisation of Orkney (far fewer Norn words were recorded there even allowing for the fact that Marwick collected his material twenty to thirty years later than Jakobsen), partly with reference to the different modes of life on the two groups of islands.

Phonologically, the late nineteenth and early twentieth-century material provides a corrective to the impression given by Low's material from Foula. We find, for example, that the majority of the features connecting Norn with Faroese and the dialects of south-west Norway are either only to be found on the West Side of Shetland and in Foula or are not represented at all (note, however, that there is some evidence for a more general diphthongisation of ON /aː/ to something like /ɔa/ (Jakobsen 1928-32:xlv), and concerning /þ/ > /h/, see above). Most significantly, perhaps, we find (seemingly — cf. Barnes 1991b:438-9) /rn/, /nː/ > /ɲ/ and /lː/ > /ʎ/ in virtually the whole of Shetland outside Foula (and possibly also the West Side, cf. Jakobsen 1928-32:lix), a development which in Norway seems to have its centre in Trøndelag. Phonological differences between Orkney and Shetland Norn are also observable. The monophthongisation of ON /ei/, /au/, /øy/, for example, was more consistent in Shetland (Marwick 1929:xlii-iv); it is also worth noting that in Orkney /rn/ and /n:/ coalesce in /n:/ and only /l:/ is palatalised (Marwick 1929:xlvi-vii).

3. THE DECLINE AND DEMISE OF NORN

There are today no speakers of Norn. At some point the language was replaced by Scots in both Orkney and Shetland. The ultimate cause is beyond doubt: the immigration of large numbers of Scots speakers into the islands in the late Middle Ages and post-Reformation period and the impignoration of 1468-9 which transferred political power from the Danish to the Scottish crown. Precisely what happened to Norn is, however, a matter about which there has been and continues to be considerable disagreement. Why did it fade away and not continue to be used side by side with Scots? When can its final demise be said to have taken place? How did it die? The main reason for the conflict of opinion is lack of data — a lack which, here as elsewhere, encourages scholars to fill the vacuum of ignorance with educated guesswork — but a significant contributory factor is the fundamental difference in approach that informs much of the guesswork — the propensity to accept or reject this or that snippet of information depending on the particular axe one has to grind.

Jakob Jakobsen, the late nineteenth-century scholar of Shetland Norn, seems to accept its demise more or less as a natural consequence of the arrival of Scots. He does not therefore spend much time considering why the two languages could not have co-existed. Nor does he appear to have any clear opinion on when Norn may have ceased to exist. He notes that *post* 1850 a few speakers were said still to be surviving, but claims their Norn 'can hardly have been of much account' (1928-32:xix). He apparently considered the idiom concerned to have been a form of Scots that was hard for the younger generation to understand because it contained a good number of Norn words they were unfamiliar with. 'Apparently' is the key word here, however, for in imposing this interpretation on Jakobsen's assertion one is probably striving for greater precision than he intended. His account of the language shift (1928-32:xiv-xx) — tendentiously described as 'the perversion of the Norn' (p.xvi) — envisages the steady infusion of Norn with Scots vocabulary and grammar, beginning in the seventeenth century and leading ultimately to a form of speech that was more Scots than Scandinavian. Nothing Jakobsen says, however, suggests he had a clear view of the point at which Scots-flavoured Norn became Norn-flavoured Scots. Certainly there is no discussion of criteria by which one could have distinguished the one language from the other.

The Jakobsen view of the shift was reinforced by Flom, who even gives an estimate of the changing ratio of Norn and Scots words in 'the total word-stock of the Shetlands' (1928-9:150). More or less the same story is told by Marwick about the displacement of Norn by Scots in Orkney. He does offer the opinion that 'the change was something more than a steady inflation of Norn with Scots words until it became more Scots than Norn', but this 'something more' turns out only to be the replacement of 'the common everyday phraseology of Norn' by 'the corresponding Scots terms of speech' (1929:xxvii).

An interpretation of the death of Shetland Norn diametrically opposed to that of Jakobsen and Flom has been offered by Laurits Rendboe (1984; 1987, especially 97-9). Much as Jakobsen, he invites us to view post-impignoration Shetland history as a story of colonial subjugation — of the 'cruel oppression' by the Scots of a society of free Scandinavian farmers, which gradually reduced the latter to a state where they were 'little better than slaves' (Rendboe 1985, Introduction:2). In his scenario, however, the Scottish incomers imposed their rule, their customs and their language on a highly reluctant and recalcitrant population. Resistance was widespread, and one of the results of the general unwillingness to bend to the Scottish yoke was that Norn remained unadulterated by Scots for as long as it was spoken by native Shetlanders — until the 1880s, according to Rendboe (accepting reports of late nineteenth-century Norn at face value), when the last speakers went to the grave (1987:6, 99).

In two articles by the present author (1989; 1991b) it has been argued that the fate of Orkney and Shetland Norn should indeed be seen in relation to the political and social history of the Northern Isles, but that it must also be judged in the light of knowledge about language death elsewhere. To these points should be added a warning against uncritical acceptance of the colonialist interpretation of post-impignoration Orkney and Shetland history, even though it is one that has enjoyed great popularity — even something of a monopoly — until quite recently. Much more is known about the past of the Northern Isles today than was the case earlier this century, and as a result there has been a significant reinterpretation of the key events.

One of the principal reinterpreters, Brian Smith, has recently turned his attention to the debate about the language shift in Shetland (1996). Smith strongly criticises Rendboe's account of Shetland history and replaces his catastrophist view of the post-impignoration situation with one in which Shetland had its good and bad years, but was in good times a thriving entrepreneurial society, and one fundamentally run by locals — people of both Scots and Norse descent, and more or less benign according to their nature and the constraints under which they operated. This rejection of the historical interpretation underlying Rendboe's account of the decline and ultimate disappearance of Norn is based on lengthy and thorough study of the primary source material (cf., e.g., Smith 1990; Ballantyne and Smith 1994) and should be given considerable weight. Smith's conception of post-impignoration Shetland society leads him to the conclusion that a form of Scots speech became established as a stable linguistic medium in the islands as early as the sixteenth century. In this and the following century, he argues, Shetlanders spoke a number of languages (Scots, Norn, Low German, Dutch — perhaps also Norwegian, we may add, which may have been learnt as a distinct form of speech) — whatever was required to safeguard their many and various commercial interests. Apart from the evidence he adduces, this seems to be in keeping with what we know of attitudes to language learning today: where the motivating factors are strong enough, people will pick up foreign tongues. Conversely, where there is little or no motivation, languages are not likely to be learnt, and in unstable bi- or multilingual situations this may lead to the abandonment of the less favoured tongue or tongues. During the seventeenth century Shetlanders' contacts with countries other than Scotland diminished, and this, Smith argues, had an effect on their linguistic proficiency. By the eighteenth century local merchant-lairds controlled commerce with the Continent, and the only language most Shetlanders would have had their attention directed to was Scots. In that situation Norn must have seemed of little relevance, and more and more people — being equally at home in Scots and Norn — stopped speaking the Scandinavian tongue. Understandably enough, given the lack of hard evidence, Smith is not specific about the date of Norn's demise, but reading between the lines one can see he has the middle of the eighteenth century in mind. He also acknowledges indirectly that for a while after the last speakers gave up the language there will have been individuals who remembered something of it.

Of the three rival interpretations of the death of Norn (chiefly Shetland Norn) that have been sketched here, the least persuasive is the Jakobsen-Flom-Marwick scenario, if for no other reason than that the imperceptible melting of one language into another they envisage seems to be without parallel. There is in addition the weakness that none of the three scholars argues a clear case for fusion; all the reader is offered is a series of inexplicit assumptions. Crucial terms such as 'Norn', 'Scots', 'dialect', 'language' etc. are used in a disconcertingly vague manner, to the extent that one is led to doubt whether the writers themselves always knew precisely what they had in mind.

Rendboe's beliefs (a) that Shetland Norn remained unadulterated by Scots as long as it continued to be spoken, and (b) that there were still speakers alive in the 1880s are based on an outmoded view of the history of the islands and uncritical acceptance of rumours reported by Jakobsen. In fairness it must be said Rendboe does his best to demonstrate the purity of Norn at different stages of its existence, but as the present author has argued on various occasions (most fully in

Barnes 1989:31-8), the evidence he adduces can often be shown to point in precisely the opposite direction.

One illustrative example concerns a verse from Unst (Jakobsen 1928-32:xviii; printed with translation and commentary on pp.49-50). This little rhyme was long held to manifest a lack of regard for Norn and consequent linguistic interference from Scots, but Rendboe — taking up an earlier suggestion that the rhymster was in fact being ironic (Stewart 1953:20) — explains it as a send-up of those who aped Scots speech (1984:75-9). Its syntax, according to him, is Norn: there is 'proper use' of the nominative, accusative, genitive and dative, the suffixed definite article is found, and the West Scandinavian word-order: noun + possessive adjective (on these and other features of Norn, cf. pp.30-31, 47-9). The inclusion of the Scots words *when*, *guid* and *ca* in this otherwise pure Norn text is done on purpose, Rendboe considers, to mimic the speech of the lad who went to Caithness and on his return could or would not keep the two languages apart. The criticism of the rhyme is not directed at a single individual, however, but at a more general malaise: the older generation is condemning the younger for mixing up Scots and Norn in their everyday speech. Thus the analysis; the weaknesses attaching to it include the following. First, we know nothing of the verse's provenance other than what Jakobsen tells us: it was from Unst and was 'said to date from the last [i.e. the eighteenth] century'. Second, considerable good will is required to recognise the appearance of four grammatical cases (cf. p.50). Third, the interpretation placed on the wording assumes that mixture of Norn and Scots had become a common enough phenomenon — the opposite conclusion from the one Rendboe champions (such a conclusion is not of course strictly necessary: the rhyme may simply imply that the lad had learnt to speak Scots).

Apart from the records of Norn itself, and the indirect testimony of literary references to the language penned at the time it was still spoken — neither of which on any dispassionate reading suggest an idiom totally unaffected by contact with Scots — there is the increasing body of knowledge about language death in general to be taken into consideration. This indicates that languages in terminal decline lose both functions and features and suffer extensive interference from the dominant tongue (cf., e.g., Dorian 1981; Schmidt 1985). Although, because of the unpredictability of human behaviour there are dangers in basing conclusions about what happened in a given linguistic situation on the outcomes af analogous situations elsewhere, such research clearly cannot be ignored.

For all the above reasons it is hard to see how Rendboe's belief in a Norn that stayed pure till the 1880s can be substantiated.

As previously indicated, it is Smith who seems to offer the most reliable picture of Shetland history, and his depiction of the linguistic situation in the islands in the sixteenth, seventeenth and eighteenth centuries sits comfortably enough with the economic and social circumstances he identifies. There is every reason to suppose that language use, then as now, was determined chiefly by the need to communicate. The concept of language as a badge of personal identity seems only to have become widespread in the nineteenth century, and has in any case tended chiefly to excite those with the leisure to ponder such matters. Smith is probably also right in his view that by the sixteenth century Scots had become a stable and well-established medium of communication in Shetland, in the sense that most people could and did use it. There is certainly little evidence of language difficulties in the islands at this or any other time. The only hint we have of a problem is the reference to Magnus norsk, a minister in Unst in the 1590s, who is said to have earned the nickname because he went to Norway 'to learn the Norse language in order to qualify himself for preaching to the Zetlanders, who at this time understood no other' (Scott 1928:298). As Scott himself points out, the reality is more likely to be that Magnus was called 'norsk' because he was a Norwegian. The best place to have learnt Norn would have been not in Norway but in his own parish in Unst. More indicative of the general state of affairs would seem to be the case of James Nisbet, a native of North Yell, and a man with Norwegian connections, who at the beginning of the seventeenth century signs letters <Jeg Jacb Nispüt for nimo>, <Jeg Jacob Nisbet for namen>, <Jeg Jacob Nisbet for navna> ?'I James Nisbet as [my] name' (the last two occurrences extant only in nineteenth-century tran-scriptions, cf. Ballantyne and Smith 1994: nos. 362, 363, 488). Here, on the face of it, is an early seventeenth-century Shetlander keen to establish a Norwegian/Danish background for himself (for whatever reason), who through linguistic ignorance has only succeeded in reveal-ing his distance from any kind of Scandinavian tradition (cf. the possible Dano-Norwegian: *Jeg haver Jacob Nisbet som navn* 'I have James Nisbet as a name' — a rather unexpected way of putting it — or more plausibly: *Mit navn/Navnet er Jacob Nisbet* 'My name/The name is James Nisbet').

The controversy about Shetland Norn has no Orcadian counterpart. In the context of a discussion on language and history in the Northern Isles, however, the present author has offered 'An interpretation of the death of Norn' which encompasses Orkney as well as Shetland (Barnes 1991b:446-56). There attention is drawn to the succession to the Orkney Earldom in 1379 of the Scots-speaking Sinclairs as well as to various other factors that suggest Scots was established earlier in the more southerly group of islands. That notwithstanding, and despite the fact that the Orcadians in the sixteenth and seventeenth centuries were more firmly in the Scottish orbit than the Shetlanders, there are indications that Norn survived in at least one or two parts of Orkney until about 1750 (Marwick 1929:224-7 reprints the principal references dating between the sixteenth century and 1814 to the existence of a Scandinavian language in the islands). Indeed, as late as 1725 there are complaints that in the Mainland parish of Sandwick 'the old broken Danish Language is used among many of the people which occasions Ignorance in the place' (Campbell 1954). Such evidence as there is thus seems to indicate that linguistic developments in Orkney to a large extent paralleled those in Shetland, though we can only guess at what motivated certain Orcadians to continue speaking Norn well into the eighteenth century.

Shetland Norn may in fact have had a number of speakers even after the middle of that century — Smith's preferred time for the language's demise — a circumstance that would fit better the later Scotticisation of Shetland. There are certainly references to Norn's being spoken in the islands in the period up to c. 1800 (cf. Stewart 1964:163-6, especially 165-6, where some of the principal sources are cited), and it is only from a nineteenth-century perspective that it is described as a language of the past. While doubt can probably be cast on these reports of late eighteenth-century Norn individually, cumulatively they carry weight. It is true that the one detailed account we have by an outside observer who came into direct contact with Shetland Norn (Low 1879:104-14) can, as Smith stresses (1996:34), be understood to mean that by the middle of the eighteenth century it had ceased to be a living language. On the other hand, this 1774 description of the linguistic situation on Foula and the West Side is ambiguous enough for the opposite inference to be drawn ('None of them can write their ancient language, and but very few speak it', 1879:105).

Having considered the evidence and the principal arguments, we are now in a position to return to the questions — why, when and how did Norn die? — posed at the outset of this investigation. While definitive answers are unobtainable, the upshot of the preceding discussion makes the following conclusions plausible.

The reason Norn died, both in Orkney and Shetland, was because the Northern Isles became more and more orientated towards Scotland. By the seventeenth century most if not all the inhabitants could speak fluent Scots, and as ties with Scandinavia, in particular Norway, weakened, the motivation to perpetuate a low-prestige vernacular with no official status or written form disappeared.

The time at which Norn died can be put at the middle of the eighteenth century in Orkney and perhaps as late as 1800 in Shetland — in the sense that it was then that the last native speakers (those whose first language had been Norn) went to the grave.

Regarding the manner in which the language died, we are on far less certain ground. Smith concludes that by the eighteenth century

Shetlanders, especially the younger generation, had turned their attention firmly towards Scotland, and so simply gave up speaking Norn (1996:35). With the help of the accumulated knowledge about language death, it is possible to expand this contention a little. Studies have indicated that there is something of a common pattern to language shift (see, e.g., Dressler and Wodak-Leodolter 1977; Rindler-Schjerve 1989). Before extinction the doomed tongue exhibits symptoms of decay and interference. It loses functions, often ending up purely as a language of the home. It also loses structures, in part at least because the usual regulatory mechanisms that help preserve language structure — institutional norms, literary tradition, correction by elders — are breaking down or are non-existent. And all the while features from the speech of the linguistically dominant group are being freely adopted. As a language decays, so its speakers desert it for the higher prestige alternative(s). This is often accomplished in the course of three generations. The first generation are native speakers of the decaying language who have learnt the new tongue for reasons of necessity, but mostly remain more proficient in the old. The next generation, largely because of greater exposure at a younger age — often from their own parents — become truly bilingual or in some cases more proficient in the new language. The children of these bilinguals are seldom exposed to the old language even in the home, and end up at best with only a very imperfect or passive knowledge of it (the second and third stages of this process can be observed at the present time in parts of the far west of Ireland). This is not to say that the first generation of Norn speakers to learn Scots in either Orkney or Shetland immediately set about transmitting it to their children to the exclusion of the traditional tongue. If that had been so, Norn would have disappeared far earlier than seems to have been the case. There was probably a period of stable bilingualism, in which succeeding generations learnt Scots for reasons of economic and social necessity, but continued using Norn as their everyday medium of communication. Then, as social and economic conditions changed, there came a generation that saw Scots as the language of the future and Norn as an unhelpful relic of the past. Such a generation would have had no incentive to perpetuate the use of their native Scandinavian and so will simply have neglected to pass Norn on to their children.

These conclusions have certain consequences for rival theories about the language shift in the Northern Isles, and it is worth emphasising them here to clear up any residual confusion. Norn and Scots were entirely separate languages and remained so for as long as Norn survived; no trained linguistic observer would have had difficulty in recognising them as distinct entities. As the low prestige language, however, Norn clearly suffered considerable interference before its

27

demise: the idea that it remained pure until the death of the last native speakers cannot be maintained.

4. TRACES OF NORN IN ORKNEY AND SHETLAND DIALECT

Even after Norn ceased to be a living language, fragments of it remained. Rhymes and snatches of conversation were remembered, and large numbers of Norn words were taken over into Scots. Most of the Scandinavian place-names of Orkney and Shetland remained intact. Jakobsen's Norn-hunting field-trip to Shetland in 1893-5 and his two brief subsequent visits resulted in a huge collection of data, including some 10,000 individual words which he considered to be of Scandinavian origin (most of this material can be found in his 1928-32 etymological dictionary). Marwick's early twentieth-century work in Orkney yielded a harvest similar in kind, but smaller. His main discovery was the existence of about 3000 probable Norn words in the Orcadian Scots of his day (published in his 1929 volume). From these collections and the analyses of them offered by Jakobsen, Marwick and later scholars, as well as from independent studies, it is possible to capture something of the Norn substratum in Orkney and Shetland speech. It should be noted, however, that there exists no definitive description of the nineteenth or twentieth-century dialects of the Northern Isles, nor those of Scotland as a totality, so any account of the traces of Norn to be found in Orkney and Shetland Scots must be somewhat impressionistic.

Claims, often contradictory, have been made about affinities in intonation between Shetland and Orkney speech and various forms of Norwegian. In the absence of contrastive studies based on precise measurements, such assertions have little value.

Regarding phonology, it is generally thought that the widespread use in Shetland of /d/ and /t/ for standard English /ð/ and /þ/ is due to the loss of [ð] and [þ] in Norn. In Orkney, too, it seems that in both Norn and Scots words original [þ] at one time appeared as /t/, but this is no longer the case. It is further possible that Norn speech habits underlie the lack of distinction between initial [hw] and [kw] in Shetland, apparently also a feature of earlier Orcadian speech. Reports of the existence of long consonants[17] in modern Shetland dialect (Catford 1957:71-2) remind one of the consonant systems of most varieties of Scandinavian outside Denmark. The vowel systems of modern Orkney and Shetland dialects, on the other hand, are Scots. It has been suggested that Norn speakers with their rich vowel system but relatively small number of consonant phonemes could more readily imitate the vocalic than the consonant distinctions of Scots (Catford 1957:73). It is nevertheless widely held that the [ø] and [ø:] sounds of the Northern-Isles dialects are a Norn relic.

On the morphological level it is to be noted that Shetland speech distinguishes between familiar *du* and formal *you*. Such a distinction is not apparently found elsewhere in Scotland, not even in Orkney, but is general in the Scandinavian-speaking world. It is also worth observing that a great many fossilised suffixes and case-endings occur in the Norn words that have survived in both Orkney and Shetland.

Syntactically, the extensive use of phrasal verbs consisting of verb + adverb has come in for comment: expressions such as Shetland *come at* 'touch', Orkney *lay off* 'chatter' are often ascribed to Norn influence. Such phrasal verbs are certainly far more common in Scandinavian languages than in English or Scots generally. The use of *he* to describe meteorological phenomena, e.g. Orkney *He'll be snaa afore long* 'There'll be snow before long' also has parallels in the Scandinavian-speaking world, notably the Faroes. Conceivably, Orkney *the're* or *de'r*, Shetland *der* 'there is, there are' may be of Norn origin (perhaps /de er/ < ON *þat er* 'it is, there is'). It has also recently been claimed (Melchers 1981:259-60) that Shetland *Minds du?* 'You remember?', *Kens du?* 'You know?' are 'obviously Norn'. Both the form *du* and the word-order are certainly suggestive of Norn origins.

It is in the lexicon that the Norn substratum is clearest in both Shetland and Orkney Scots. It should however be remembered that the 10,000 words in Jakobsen 1928-32 and the 3000 in Marwick 1929 represent what the two scholars were able to elicit from informants — many of them of considerable age — some 70 to 100 years ago. Enquiries have indicated that in Shetland, at least, only about a tenth of the total are now likely to be recognised, and the same is doubtless true of Orkney. Nevertheless, it is clear that the modern dialects of both groups of islands preserve a sizeable body of words of Norn origin. These tend to be restricted to particular areas of the vocabulary and many writers on the subject attempt a rough categorisation. The categories that emerge, however, are often based on the Norn word-stocks of Jakobsen and Marwick, in spite of recognition that developments in Orkney and Shetland society over the last 150-200 years make any systematisation based on this material largely invalid for the modern dialects. It would be wrong to think, for example, that an important area of Shetland speech for the preservation of Norn words is the taboo language of fishermen, since this system of oblique references is now no longer in use. Melchers (1981:260b), writing exclusively about present-day speech, lists the following areas of vocabulary as being particularly rich in Norn words: types of wind and weather; flowers and plants; animals; seasons and holidays; food; tools; materials and colours; movement; whims, ludicrous behaviour, unbalanced states of mind, qualities.

In conclusion it is worth reiterating that the vast majority of place-names in Orkney and Shetland are of Scandinavian origin. A recent study of the place-names of Foula showed there to be about 80 Scots or hybrid names to 800 Norn (Stewart 1970:318-19). It is likely that the proportion would be similar throughout the Northern Isles.

THE PRINCIPAL FEATURES OF NORN[18]

Norn was a Scandinavian language, descended like Danish, Faroese, Icelandic, Norwegian and Swedish from the so-called Common Scandinavian of the Viking Age. Traditionally Common Scandinavian is reckoned to have split into an eastern and a western branch, often called Old East Scandinavian (or Old East Norse) and Old West Scandinavian (Old West Norse). The eastern branch comprised Danish and Swedish, and the western Norwegian and its daughter languages: Faroese, Icelandic and Norn. Scandinavian languages themselves are a branch of Germanic, which is a sub-group of the Indo-European language family. Germanic languages, apart from Scandinavian, include Dutch, German and English, and the now extinct Gothic (see further König and van der Auwera 1994).

Languages that are related have shared features — the closer the relationship, the more features they will normally have in common. Some of the more easily recognised features that mark Norn out as Germanic and Scandinavian are the following.

Like all Germanic languages (except some colonial varieties), Norn had two basic tenses of the verb: present and past (cf. English *writes — wrote, starts — started*), and three moods: indicative, subjunctive and imperative (English he *comes*, I suggest that he *come*, *come!*). It also distinguished between strong and weak verb conjugations (those in which the past tense is formed by vowel change and those where a suffix is employed, cf. *wrote* as opposed to *started*). Norn also inherited a number of features that were once common to all Germanic languages but which have since disappeared from some. (1) Two numbers (singular and plural), three genders (masculine, feminine, neuter) and four cases (nominative, accusative, genitive, dative) were marked in nouns, pronouns and adjectives (which 'agreed' with each other, i.e., modifiers like adjectives took their number, gender and case from the word they modified). (2) There was a distinction between strong and weak adjective declension depending on function (cf. German *ein guter Mann* 'a good man' — indefinite, *der gute Mann* 'the good man' — definite). (3) There was personal inflexion in the verb (as in older English *I go — thou goest — he goeth*, and still *you go — he goes*). (4) Strong and weak nouns were distinguished (essentially this means two fundamentally different types of declension occurred, cf. German *der Mann* (nom.) — *den Mann* (acc.) — *des Mannes* (gen.) — *dem Mann(e)* (dat.) 'the man', but *der Mensch — den Mensch(en) — des Menschen — dem Mensch(en)* 'the person'). (5) The passive was expressed by the use of an auxiliary verb + the past participle (cf. English *it was taken* as opposed to the active *John took it*).

In common with virtually all varieties of Scandinavian, Norn had a suffixed definite article (cf. Norwegian *mannen* 'man-the', *huset* 'house-the'), and in common with all an *-sk* verb ending (later *-st*, East Scandinavian *-s*), which had reflexive, reciprocal, passive and sundry other functions (cf. Faroese *seta* 'set, put, seat', *setast* 'seat oneself [i.e., sit down]'). Norn often indicated number and case by changes in the root vowel instead of, or as well as, by endings (a more regular feature in Old Norse than in other Germanic languages). It also shared with Scandinavian languages generally an infinitive that ended in a vowel (*-a* in Norn), as well as vowel endings in weak nouns and adjectives (rather than *-n*, the regular ending in earlier Germanic for all three categories). Pan-Scandinavian too, but not pan-Germanic, were the pronouns for 'some(one), any(one)' (ON *nǫkkurr*, Dan. *nogen*, Far. *nakar* etc.), 'no one, none' (ON *engi*, Dan. *ingen*, Far. *eingin* etc.) and 'he' and 'she' (ON *hann/hon*, Dan. *han/hun*, Far. *hann/hon* etc.) — all of which were part of Norn. Other personal pronouns, inherited from Germanic, developed specifically — and varying — Scandinavian forms, and Norn also had its range of these (see below and p.17).

Certain features of Norn were peculiar to West Scandinavian. In particular may be noted: the dative plural form of the definite article *-unum*; the second person plural verbal ending *-ð*; vowel change in the present singular indicative and past subjunctive of verbs, cf. Old West Scandinavian *taka* '[to] take' — *tekr* 'takes', *tók* 'took [indicative]' — *tœki* 'took [subjunctive]'; the forms of a number of personal pronouns, e.g. *ek* 'I', *vér* 'we', (*þ*)*ér* 'you [pl.]'. Originally Common Scandinavian, but ultimately preserved only in the west was the word-order noun + possessive adjective, cf. Faroese *drongur mín* 'boy my [i.e., my boy]', Norwegian *huset hennes* 'house-the her [i.e., her house]'.

ANNOTATED TEXTS

Runic Inscriptions

Cunningsburgh III, Shetland

Transliteration:[19]
](x)þi****(+)*ftir+foþur(·)sin(:)þurbio(r)[

Text:
...þenna eptir fǫður sinn, Þorbjǫrn.

Translation:
(1) Literal: '...this after father his, Þorbjǫrn.'
(2) Idiomatic: '[NN raised/made] this [stone] in memory of Þorbjǫrn, his father.'

A brief discussion of this and other Orkney and Shetland inscriptions will be found in Olsen 1954:158-69 (cf. also Barnes 1993). Cunningsburgh III seems to have been a memorial stone of common Viking-Age type, but only the conclusion of the inscription now survives.

Sanday, Orkney

Transliteration:
]nxin:āska**:r[

Text:
...(?sinn), en Ásgeirr/Áskell (?)reist.

Translation:
'...his/her/their [following the designation of a dead relation], but Ásgeirr/Áskell carved [the runes].'

A preliminary notice of this recently-discovered inscription is given by Barnes and Page (1996:12). It is a mere fragment, on a broken piece of

The Sanday fragment. *Photo: Michael P. Barnes*

stone, but appears originally to have been part of a Viking-Age memorial inscription, the first one of its kind discovered in Orkney. Note that the runes run along the narrow edge, the almost universal practice on Norwegian commemorative rune stones.

Orphir I, Orkney

Transliteration:
ikirkirkiakoþ(li)ufs...[

Text:
Engi er kirkja goði ljúf (?)sem...

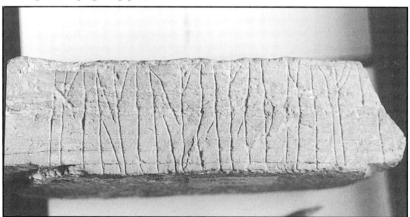

The Orphir stone *Photo: Michael P. Barnes*
(taken by permission of Tankerness House Museum, Kirkwall)

Translation:
(1) Literal: 'No is church to God [dat.] pleasing as...'
(2) Idiomatic: 'No church is [as] pleasing to God as [this].'

The inscription is discussed by Hagland (1993:370-73). It is on a loose piece of stone found close to the ruins of the round church at Orphir, and is thought to be a medieval graffito extolling the virtues of the building.

Maeshowe No. 9, Orkney

Transliteration:
inkibiorh·hinfahra·æhkia
mọrhk·kona·hæfïr·farït·lu(t)inhïrmihkiloflatï
ærlikr

Text:
Ingibjǫrg, hin fagra ekkja. Mǫrg kona hefir farit lút inn hér. Mikill ofláti. Erlingr.

Translation:
'Ingibjǫrg, the fair widow. Many a woman has gone stooping in here. A great show-off. Erlingr.' [Note that ON has no indefinite article.]

Part of Maeshowe inscription No. 9.   *Photo: Bengt A. Lundberg, Central Board of National Antiquities, Stockholm*

Maeshowe No. 20, Orkney

Transliteration:
þisarrunar
ristsamaþr·ïr·runstrïr·fyrir
uæstanhaf
mæþ·þæiriøhsï·ïratï·kǫukr·trænilsonrfyrir·sunanlant

Text:
Þessar rúnar reist sá maðr, er rúnstr er fyrir vestan haf, með þeiri øxi, er átti Gaukr Trandilssonr fyrir sunnan land.

Translation:
(1) Literal: 'These runes carved that man who most runic is west of ocean, with that axe which owned Gaukr Trandilssonr south of land.'
(2) Idiomatic: 'The man who is most skilled in runes west of the ocean carved these runes with the axe which Gaukr Trandilssonr owned in the south of the country [Iceland].'

The Maeshowe inscriptions are edited in Barnes 1994, where they are interpreted as light-hearted medieval graffiti. It has been generally assumed (with good reason) that most or all of them were carved in the 1150s in connection with a crusade mounted by the Orkney earl, Rǫgnvaldr Kali. A considerable number of people, including many Norwegians, gathered in Orkney in the winter of 1150-51 before setting out for the Holy Land. There are references in *Orkneyinga saga* to their unruly behaviour, and two of the Maeshowe carvings make the specific claim that crusaders broke into the cairn. Some of the inscriptions may date from the crusaders' return or later.

It is not known who the Ingibjǫrg or Erlingr mentioned in No. 9 are, though there has been speculation about both. Gaukr Trandilssonr, whose axe is declared to be the tool with which No. 20 was cut, is familiar from Icelandic sources. He is said to have lived at Stöng in southern Iceland in the tenth century and to have been slain by his foster brother, Ásgrímr Ellliða-Grímssonr (see Einar Ól. Sveinsson 1954:72-3, 371, chs. 26, 139).

Documents in the Roman Alphabet
Shetland 1299

Text:

Allum þeim mannum sem þetta bref sia eða heyra senda allir logðingis-menn af hiatlandi. Queðiu. Guðs. ok sina þat se yðr kunnikt at a þui are er liðit uar [fra] burd uars herra ihu xpi. M^O. CC^O. XC^O. ok IX° uetr. let

herra þorualldr þoris son bera uitni fyr oss a logþingi. orð þau sem
ragnhilldr simunar ðottir hafði talat. baro þeir sua uitni Juar bondi aeiði
ok haralldr iborgarfirði at þeir uoro hia þui istofvni ahertogabœnvm
ipapey manadagenn idymbildaga uiku er Ragnhilldr tok sua til orða at
breka sætr uar ecki ileigu með skat jorðu upi ihusi ok hertogin skylldi
taka fulla leigo þot breka sætr uæri ecki með. en þorualldr sagði. her hafa
sua margir goðir menn um uellt sem var þorkell inesi herra Eirikr sigurðr
erkidiakn herra Eindriði ok margir aðrir dugandi menn þeir er hafðo
umboð mins herra hertogans huilika landskylld þeir toko hanom til
handa i papey. fyr mer. Ragnhilldr suaraði. ek œnti ecki Eindriða œrum.
er hann líop ustan or noregi ok uissi alldri fagnat. en þer allir sem uissuð
þa hafa suikit hertogann. en sueinn prestr ok halfdan abruarsætri baro
sua at þeir uoro hia þui ummorgonen eftir atysdagenn uti ituninu
afyrsagdum bœ er Ragnhilldr sagði sua til herra þorualldar at þu skallt
ecki uera minn iudás. þot þu ser hertogans ok þessi orð uitnadi herra
þorualldr aalla þa sem nær uoro. Profaz ok alldri meiri uerðavrar a allri
papey en sua sem iafnan hefir gengit at fyrnd. mork gullz brendri með
uelltu iorðu huert penings land. en ilandskylld halfs annars mælis uerð
af huerri mork brendri ok er þa .ij. salld ahueriv penings landi. Nu af þui
at herra þorvalldr ok þeir fleiri sem hon hafði til talat. uilia ganga logligri
dul firir sialfum hertoganum. þa gafvm uer þetta rannzaks bref til uars
virðulegs herra hertogans um fyr sogd malefni. ok þui at uer hofdum eigi
logþinngis insigli þa settu þessir af uarum kumpanum sin insigli fyr þetta
bref til sannz uitnis burdar. herra Eirikr ungi. Gregorius benedictz son
Juar sperra Magnus hogna son Erlendr geirmundar son gunni agnipum.
Erlendr alfeitr.

Translation:
To all the men who see or hear this letter, all the lawthingmen of
Shetland send God's greeting and their own. Be it known to you that, in
the year when 1299 winters had passed from the birth of our Lord Jesus
Christ, herra Þorualldr Þorisson had testimony brought before us at the
lawthing [concerning] the words spoken by Ragnhilldr Simunardottir.
   Iuarr bondi a Æiði and Haralldr i Borgarfirði bore witness that they
were present in the main building of the ducal farm in Papey [i.e. Papa
Stour], on Monday in Passion Week, when Ragnhilldr spoke saying that
Brekasætr was not rented out as part of the tributary property of the
house, and the duke should take full rent though Brekasætr were not
included. But Þorualldr said: 'So many good men have dealt with this,
Þorkell i Nesi, herra Eirikr, Archdeacon Sigurðr, herra Eindriði, and
many other able men who had full authority from my lord the duke
concerning the amount of rent they took for him in Papey on my behalf.'
Ragnhilldr answered: 'I gave no heed to the mad Eindriði, when he ran

away from Norway hither and never knew a day's happiness; but all of you who knew have deceived the duke.'

But Sueinn the priest and Halfdan a Bruarsætri bore witness that they were present the next morning, on Tuesday, out in the toon of the aforesaid farm, when Ragnhilldr said to herra Þorualldr: 'You shall not be my Judas, though you be Judas to the duke.' Herra Þorualldr called all those present as witnesses of these words.

[Herewith] it is also demonstrated that there [has] never [been] greater payment from the whole of Papey than that which has been common from of old: a mark of refined gold for every cultivated pennyland, and in rent 1½ mælar from every refined mark, and there are then 2 sáld on every pennyland.

Now, since herra Þorualldr and the others she had spoken to wish to swear a legal oath of denial [about her accusations] before the duke himself, we gave this letter of enquiry to our noble lord the duke about the aforesaid matters, and because we had no lawthing seal the following of our companions set their seals on this letter by way of confirmation: herra Eirikr ungi, Gregorius Benedictzson, Juar sperra, Magnus Hognason, Erlendr Geirmundarson, Gunni a Gnipum, Erlendr alfeitr.

The language of this document is Old Norwegian. The only possible "Island" forms are <ustan> 'from the east' for usual *austan* (cf. p.13) and <uelltu iorðu> 'cultivated land', an apparent compound *veltujǫrð*, otherwise unrecorded (but cf. Faroese *velta* 'cultivate'). 'Lawthingmen' are members of the chief court of Shetland. A 'pennyland' is a measurement of arable land; *sáld* and *mælir* are measurements of capacity for grain, the *sáld* being the greater. For further explanations of technical terms found in medieval Shetland documents, see Ballantyne and Smith forthcoming.

Kirkwall, 25 May 1369

Text:

Jn nomine domini Amen. Þessre dentura ber vitni vm satmal jmillum virðulex herra ok andelex fadr herra Willialms með guds nad biscup j Orkneyum ok Hiatlanð af æin halfuo ok af annarre halfuo heidrlegr man ok vel boren Hakon Jonsson Var þitta satmal giort j millum þeira godra mana vm þat sundrþyke sem j millum þeira var ok þeira manna j ymissum lutum þessre men fyriruerande sira Willialmr af Bucchan erkindiakin j Orkneyum sira Valter af Bucchan kannugkr j samastað sira Jon Proktur. sira Richard af Rollissey. sira Cristen af Teyn sira Cristen af Sanday sira Willialmr Wod Thomas Arland. Fergus af Rosce. Henri

Orkney diploma of 1369.

Photo: The Arnamagnæan Institute, Copenhagen (Dipl. Norv. Fasc. 100, 5)

Willialms Jon af Orkneyum Willialmr Stormr Jon af Boduel Jon Robertsson Adam af Mwre. Gudbrand Andrsson Sighurdr af Pappley Jon Sincler Patrik Kaldar Dunkan af Karmkors Bube Skinner Willialmr Eruin Jon af Dunray Olaue Skutt. att herra biscup aa sina vengna ok Hakon aa sina halfuo vnðr loghdo sik likamleghom með suornom æide att þeira skilde hafua ok vbryghdelegha halda þat ær þeir fyrnemd men saghdo þeir j millum. War þitta itt frista at herra biscup skild vp luga hundra tolfuo ret gull penninga ok æin ok tuttv ær noblis æita. ok sua mikit smior sem fyrsagdr herra biskup hafue kyr sett j hans geymslo varum herra koninghenum till handa. Var sua skipat þat herra biskup skilde af henda Hakone fyrsagda gull peninga ok hann skilde þar með gera sem hann vill suarra fyrir varum herra koninghenum. Ok sua vm þa men ok þeira godz sem herra biscup let takka ok in setia till ret ransakz vm þeira brot. þa men skide hann vp gifua lidugha till Hakonar ok þeir godz. jam vel þat ær tekit var fra lerdum monnum som leikum j Orkneyum ok Hiatlanð godz þat sem Hakon aate. vpp a þan hatt at Hakone ok hans men skullu aptir gefua alt þat godz ær hann ok hans men hafua tekit af herra biscup monnum lerdum ok leikum j Orkneyum ok Hiatlanð. Ok sua var skipat ok samþykt þat herra biscup ok hin rikest men j Orkneyum ok Hiatlanð skullu frist ok fremst j ollum rað vera hedan af. þat sem vardar koninghenum kyrkiune ok almughanum epptir loghum ok landzsidum Ok herra biskup skall hafua goda men jnlenzka j Orkneyum ok Hiatlanð at þiona sik epptir þui sem adrer biscupar halfua haft ok hafua j Norex koningx rike. Sua skall herra biscup ok hans vndr men frealslegha nita jurisdiccionem af heilagre kyrkiu baðe lerdr ok

38

leikar fir vtan lette af Hakone æda hans manna. Ok sua fellir at nokkrar biscup men verda brotleghar j mote Hakone monnum þa skullum þeira beta þeira brot epptir loghum ok landzsið vspellað þeira satmal. Ok ef sua fellir at nokkrar Hakonar men vera brutlegha j mote herra biscup monnum þa skullu þeira beta þeira brut sem fyrir seghir vtan þeir badr vilia betr giort hafua sine j millum. Ok sua skall herra biscupen vera skadalaus klerkar leikmen ok landbular fir Hakone ok hans monnum vtan með loghum. Sua skall Hakone hans men ok landbular vera skadalausar fyr herra biskupe ok hans monnum vtan með loghum. Ok var skipat ok samþykt j millum þeira herra biscup ok Hakone att huor þeira skall vera annars vin j ollum retum erendum. firir þeira liftima með vbridilegha vinatu. En huor þeira sem rifuir æda rofsmen till fer. þa skall hann luga hundrað pund ensk ok æin man till gamil Romsc. Ok till sanenda her vm herra biscup jnsigle er set till þis ludz in denture sem Hakon hefuir með jnsigle fyrsagdra manna. Ok jnsigle Hakonar er set till þis lutar sem herra biscup hefuir hia ser með jnsiglum fyrsagdra manna. Er skriuad var j Kyrkiuvaghe jn festo sancti Vrbani pape. Anno domini M^O. CCC^O. LX^{mo}. nono.

In the above capital and lower case letters are distributed according to modern practice since it is for the most part impossible to distinguish the one from the other.

Translation:
In the name of the Lord, Amen. This indenture bears witness to an agreement between the noble lord and spiritual father herra Willialmr, by the grace of God Bishop of Orkney and Shetland, on the one side, and on the other the honourable and well-born man Hakon Jonsson. This agreement was made between those good men about the quarrels that existed between them and their men in various matters, in the presence of these men: sira Willialmr of Bucchan, Archdeacon of Orkney, sira Valter of Bucchan, canon in the same place, sira Jon Proktur, sira Richard of Rollissey [i.e. Rousay], sira Cristen of Teyn, sira Cristen of Sanday, sira Willialmr Wod, Thomas Arland, Fergus of Rosc, Henri Willialms, Jon of Orkney, Willialmr Stormr, Jon of Boduel, Jon Robertsson, Adam of Mwre, Gudbrandr Andrsson, Sighurdr of Pappley, Jon Sincler, Patrikr Kaldar, Dunkan of Karmkors, Bube Skinner, Willialmr Eruin, Jon of Dunray, Olaue Skutt. The lord bishop on his own behalf and Hakon on his pledged themselves with a bodily oath [i.e. *corporale juramentum*] to accept and inviolably keep what the aforesaid men decided concerning the matters between them.
This was the first that the lord bishop should pay 141 gold coins [of the kind] which are called nobles, and as much butter as the aforesaid lord bishop had impounded in his store, to our lord the king. It was

determined that the lord bishop should deliver the aforesaid gold coins to Hakon, and he should use them in such a way as he is prepared to answer for to our lord the king.

And as for the men and their property whom the lord bishop had seized and jailed for [i.e. in order to carry out] a legal investigation into their crimes, those men he was to release into Hakon's hands, and their property — that which was taken from clerics and laymen alike in Orkney and Shetland, [and] the property which Hakon owned; subject to Hakon and his men giving back all that property which he and his men have taken from the lord bishop's men, clerics and laymen, in Orkney and Shetland.

It was also arranged and agreed that the lord bishop and the most powerful men in Orkney and Shetland shall, primarily, be in all counsels henceforth affecting the king, the church and the people, in accordance with the laws and customs of the land.

And the lord bishop shall have good native men to serve him in Orkney and Shetland, as other bishops have had and have in the realm of the King of Norway.

Further, the lord bishop and his subjects shall enjoy freely the jurisdiction of the holy church, both clerics and laymen, without hindrance from Hakon or his men. And [if] it happens that any of the bishop's men trespass against Hakon's men, they shall atone for their crime in accordance with the laws and custom of the land without detriment to the agreement between them. And if it happens that any of Hakon's men trespass against the lord bishop's men, they shall atone for their crime as previously stated, unless they both come to some better understanding between them. And the lord bishop, clerics, laymen and tenants shall be safe from Hakon and his men, except by law. Similarly, Hakon, his men and tenants shall be safe from the lord bishop and his men except by law.

And it was arranged and agreed between the lord bishop and Hakon that each shall be the other's friend in all just matters for their lifetime, with steadfast friendship. But whichever of them reverses [this agreement] or gets others to do so, he shall pay a hundred English pounds and [send] a man to old Rome.

And in confirmation hereof the seal of the lord bishop is set on that part of the indenture which Hakon has, with the seals of the aforesaid men, and Hakon's seal is set on that part which the lord bishop has with him, with the seals of the aforesaid men. Which [document] was written in Kyrkiuvaghr on the feast day of the holy Pope Urban, in the year of our Lord 1369.

The language is once again Old Norwegian, but there are a great many ungrammatical constructions. If the scribe was a native Orcadian, that would indicate he was no longer wholly familiar with the Old Norse inflexional system, which might in turn suggest that by the middle of the fourteenth century the system had undergone considerable change in the local idiom. There is no other evidence to support the assumption of radical change, but then there are few pointers at all to how Scandinavian speech developed in Orkney. Another, and perhaps more likely, explanation of the aberrant constructions is that the letter was written by a non-native who had learnt some form of West Scandinavian, but only imperfectly. While such a person would most probably have been trained to write the language in Norway (cf. p.11), they might well have learnt to speak it in Orkney, which could explain the unusual spellings — presumably reflecting phonological divergence — scattered throughout the letter (examples are given on pp.13-15). Among the many ungrammatical constructions may be noted: <hin rikest men> for ON *hinir ríkustu menn* (nom. m. pl.) 'the most powerful men'; <at nokkrar Hakonar men vera brutlegha> for *at nǫkkurir Hákonar menn verða brotlegir* — with apparent feminine <nokkrar> and accusative <brutlegha> modifying nominative masculine <men> — 'that any of Hakon's men trespass'; <þa skullum þeira heta þeira brot> for *þá skulu þeir bœta brot sín* — with first for third person plural verb, and genitive <þeira> once as subject (instead of nominative) and once as reflexive (instead of the usual *sín*) — 'then they shall atone for their crime'.

    <hundra tolfuo ret> is a way of writing *hundrað tólfrœtt* 'a duodecimal hundred', i.e. 120. 'Old Rome' seems to be a reference to Rome itself as opposed to Avignon, where the popes resided from approximately 1305 to 1375.

Gerde, Redeførd [i.e. Reafirth] parish, Yell, 4 December 1586

Text:
Anno 1586 paa thenn fierde dag December wore wÿ effther skriffne ÿ gerde ÿ Redeførd sogenn thett er att sige willom monssønn til gerde Laurettis mand ÿ ønÿst och wmbos mand for effter skriffne brødre Aassi och gilbertt skott och medt honnom Salamom schott och Lauffrens schott fornemde aassi och gÿlberts brøder paa faderside och medt them peder nÿsbitt til Kirckebusted och Jamis Burgar sergenn ÿ Jella och mons nÿsbitt till Congne saatther giøre witterligt for alle att oppaa forskriffne Dag hørde wÿ och soge ein wenligh forligelse ÿ mellom Aassi schott och gÿlbert schott paa then enne side och Jamis nÿsbitt theris støffader paa then andre side om cont och regenskab them ÿ mellom ÿ fraa thenn thime som fornemde Jamis nÿsbi[tt] giffte forne Aassi och gilberts moder witt naffn Kathrina mathisdaatter baade om landskÿld och al andenn thingh som wor them ÿmellom och wor thette theris forligelse att forskriffne aassi wnder mette och opbaar baade sinn egenn partt och sin broders gÿlberts schott paartt ÿ fraa fornne Jamis nÿsbitt och effther thÿ

41

att forne Jamis haffde
bÿct en nÿ stoffue och
andre huus huar ing-
en wor till forne,
forne aassi och gil-
bertt till gode Daa
funne wÿ forskriffne
mend ÿmellom gud
och oss att forne
Jamis haffde giørtt
well och haffde mere
wdlagt och kostidt paa
forskriffnne huus en
hand them skÿldigh
wor menn effther thÿ
att the wenlige forlig-
this medt hand och
mund, wilde fornende
Jamis icke recne thett
dÿriste menn att
huert skulde stande
paa andit hussene
som hand haffde bÿct
och skyldem som hand
them wor skyldigh
men for kornitt som
forne Jamis wnder
mette witt och opbaar
medt theris moder
och forne aassi och
gilbert medt theris

Shetland diploma of 1586.
Photo: Scottish Record Office (document RH6/2869)

sÿster Besi schott wore føde paa Daa funne vÿ forne mend saa att ÿ huadt
aar heller stund att forne Jamis nÿsbi[tt] affløtther theris jord ÿ
forskriffne gierde Daa skall forne Jamis vd winne thett helle tuun medt
sitt egitt korn, folck och redskab och sidenn giffue forne aassi och gilbert
och Besi then enne halffue part aff kornitt och thenn andre halffue till
sigh sielff att saa er ÿ sandhedt her wnder woris handskriffter och insigler
och mercker och efftherdi att forne aassi och gilbertt schott aager icke
insigle aff theris egitt haffuer the beger[t] hederlige mand och gode wenn
att besegle thette breff for thenn som er h. mons norsko minister ÿ Jella
aar och dag som forre siger. Jegh Laurens skott metth min handtt.

Translation:
In the year 1586 on the fourth day of December, we the following were in
Gerde in Redeførd parish: that is to say, Willom Monssønn of Gerde,

42

parochial officer in Ønyst, and representative of the following brothers: Aassi and Gilbertt Skott, and with him Salamom Schott and Lauffrens Schott, brothers of the aforementioned Aassi and Gylbert on their father's side, and with them Peder Nysbitt of Kirckebusted and Jamis Burgar, sergeant in Jella, and Mons Nysbitt of Congnesaatther. [We] make known to all that on the aforesaid day we heard and saw a friendly agreement between Aassi Schott and Gylbert Schott on the one side and Jamis Nysbitt, their stepfather, on the other side, about count and reckoning between them from the time that the aforementioned Jamis Nysbitt married the mother of the aforementioned Aassi and Gilbert, Kathrina Mathisdaatter by name, both as regards rent and all other matters that were between them. And this was their agreement: that the aforesaid Aassi obtained and received both his own share and his brother Gylbert Schott's share, from the aforementioned Jamis Nysbitt; and since the aforementioned Jamis had built a new house and other buildings where none were before, for the benefit of the aforementioned Aassi and Gilbertt, so we, the aforesaid men, judged before God and ourselves that the aforementioned Jamis had acted well, and had used and spent more on the aforesaid buildings than he owed them. But since they made a friendly agreement with hand and mouth, the aforementioned Jamis would not reckon the highest price, but that each should cancel the other out, the buildings he had put up and the rent which he owed them. But regarding the corn which the aforementioned Jamis obtained with and received with their mother, and the aforementioned Aassi and Gilbert, with their sister, Besi Schott, were fed with, we, the aforementioned men, determined that in whatever year or hour the aforementioned Jamis Nysbitt moves from their land in the aforesaid Gierde, then the aforementioned Jamis shall work the whole infield with his own corn, people and tools, and thereupon give to the aforementioned Aassi and Gilbert and Besi the one half share of the corn, and the other half to himself.

[To confirm] that the above is true [we append] here below our signatures and seals and marks, and since the aforementioned Aassi and Gilbertt Schott do not have seals of their own, they have asked the honourable man and good friend, Mr Mons norsko, minister in Jella, to seal this letter for them, [made] in the year and on the day stated above. [Signed] I Laurens Skott, with my hand.

This document is in Danish, which by about 1530 had become the sole written medium of Norway. The inflexional system of Old Norse has disappeared completely, and been replaced by a grammatical structure not unlike that of modern Danish, Norwegian and Swedish. The document contains a few features that are clearly local, not least the Scots loan-words: <sergenn> 'sergeant', <cont> 'count', and

<minister>. In addition, the construction <aff theris egitt> seems to derive from the Scots *of thair awen*. The confusion of final /m/ and /n/ is discussed on p.15. Concerning <mons norsko>, see p.25.

Together these three public documents show the very close affinity of the written Scandinavian of the Northern Isles to that of Norway. The Shetland letter of 1299 is in impeccable Old Norwegian (bar two possible 'Island' forms). Even though the 1369 Orkney indenture exhibits a number of aberrant constructions, the language is still fundamentally Old Norwegian — just as it was in Norway in the third quarter of the fourteenth century. Thereafter a change sets in, and written Norwegian is subject first to Swedish and then increasingly heavy Danish influence. By the early sixteenth century Norwegian has to all intents and purposes ceased to exist as a written idiom. It has been superseded by Danish, a circumstance that is faithfully reflected in the 1586 document from Yell.

Not only do Orkney and Shetland documents mirror general linguistic trends in Norway, they are also dependent on Norwegian, and subsequently Danish, models for their layout and stock of formulaic expressions.

Records of Spoken Norn

The *Hildina* ballad vv.1-4, 20-23

Text:

1. Da vara Iarlin d' Orkneyar
   For frinda sin spir de ro
   Whirdè ane skildè meun
   Our glas buryon burtaga.

2. Or vanna ro eidnar fuo
   Tega du meun our glas buryon
   Kere friendè min yamna meun
   Eso vrildan stiende gede min vara to din.

3. Yom keimir eullingin
   Fro liene burt
   Asta vaar hon fruen Hildina
   Hemi stu mer stien.

4. Whar an yaar elonden
   Ita kan sadnast wo
   An scal vara keindè
   Wo osta tre sin reithin ridna dar fro.

Da vara Iarlin d'Orkneyar
For frinda sin spur de ro
Whirde ane shilde meun
Our glas buryon burtaga.
Or vanna ro eidnar feo
Tega du meun our glas buryon
Kere friende min yamna meun
Eso vrildan stiende gede min vara to din.
Yom keimir cullingin
Fro liene burt
Asta vaar hon fruen Hildina
Kemi slu mar slien.
4. Whar an yaar slonden
Ita han sadnast wo
An scal vara huendè
Wo osta bre sin seithin ridna dar fro.

Verses 1-4 of the *Hildina* ballad. *Reproduced with permission from Edinburgh University Library (manuscript La.III.580 fols 101-2)*

20.   Nu fruna Hildina
On genger e vadlin fram
Fy di yera da ov man dum
Dora di spidlaikè mire man.

21.   Nu sware an Hiluge
Crego gevan a scam
Gayer an Iarlen frinde
Din an u fadlin in

22.   Nu fac an Iarlen dahuge
Dar min de an engin gro
An cast ans huge ei
Fong ednar u vax hedne mere neo.

23. Di lava mir gugna
Yift bal yagh fur o lande
Gipt mer nu fruan Hildina
Vath godle u fasta bande

Translation:

1. It was the earl of Orkney, asked advice of his kinsman: whether he should take the maiden out of the glass palace.

2. Get [her] out of her difficulties. 'If you take the maiden out of the glass palace, my dear kinsman, for as long as this world remains you will be remembered.' [The last three lines of verse 2 in the manuscript seem to represent a complete four-line stanza; line 1 may be the refrain, or, possibly, the last line of verse 1, in which case 'take...out of the glass palace' is the refrain.]

3. Home comes the lord back from the naval expedition; away was the lady Hildina, at home stands her stepmother.

4. 'Whatever country he is in who can be shown to have done this, he shall be hung on the highest tree which runs from its roots.'

20. Now the lady Hildina, she goes forward onto the field [of battle]: 'Father, do it out of your humanity — do not waste the lives of more men.'

21. Now Hiluge answers — God confound him! 'As soon as the earl, your friend, has fallen too.'

22. Now the earl received his death blow, no one there could heal him. He [Hiluge] threw his [the earl's] head into her arms, and her mood grew fiercer still.

23. [Hiluge said] 'You promised me marriage(?) if bold I left the country. Now give me the lady Hildina with gold and betrothal vows.'

The full text of the ballad, as well as an account of the circumstances in which it was collected, will be found in Low 1879:lvi, 95-114. A complete English verse translation was made by W.G. Collingwood and published in 1908. No commentary is available in English; the best is still Hægstad 1900, in Norwegian. Low knew no Scandinavian, so he used his English, and apparently also French, spelling habits to record the sounds he

46

heard; hence such forms as <Fy>, probably /fa:i/, 'father', <meun>, probably /mø:n/, 'the maiden'.

The *Hildina* ballad illustrates many of the linguistic features outlined on pp.30-31.

Tense: <yaar> 'is' v.4, pres.; <vaar> 'was' v.3, past.

Mood: <spir de> 'asked' v.1, indic.; <gevan a> [i.e. geve (h)ono(n)] '[let God] give him' v.21, subj.; <Gipt> 'give in marriage' v.23, imp.

Number: <lande> 'country' v.23, sg.; <londen> 'countries' v.4, pl.

Gender: <Iarlin> 'earl' v.1, m.; <dahuge> 'death blow' v.22, n.; <Eso> 'this' v.2, f.; <Ita> 'this' v.4, n.

Cases: <an> 'he' v.4, nom.; <an> 'him' v.22, acc.; <ans> 'his' v.22, gen. [used as possessive]; <an a> [i.e. (h)ono(n)] 'him' v.21, dat. Cf. also: <din> 'you' v.2, gen.; <mer> '[to] me' v.23, dat.; <liene> 'the naval expedition' v.3, dat.; <godle> 'gold' v.23, dat.

Agreement: <frinda sin> 'his kinsman' v.1, both words are acc. m. sg.; <Iarlen...fadlin> 'the earl...fallen' v.21, both words are nom. m. sg.

Strong and weak adjectives: <fadlin> 'fallen' v.21, strong; <Kere> 'dear' v.2, weak; <osta> 'highest' v.4, weak.

Verb inflexion: <keimir> 'comes' v.3, sg.; <yera> 'do' v.20, pl. Personal inflexion does not seem to occur in the verses cited.

Voice: <Tega> 'take' v.2, active; <vara keindè> 'be hung', v.4, passive.

Suffixed definite article: <Iarlin> 'the earl' v.1; <vadlin>'the field' v.20; <dahuge> 'the death blow' v.22.

Verb form in -*st*: <sadnast> 'be proved', v.4.

Root vowel alternation: <lande> 'country' v.23; <londen> 'countries' v.4.

Infinitive and weak adjective end in a vowel: <burtaga> 'take away' v.1, inf.; <osta> 'highest' v.4, weak adj.

Vowel change in present singular: <burtaga> 'take away' v.1, inf.; <Tega> 'take' v.2, pres. sg.

Scandinavian pronouns: see 'Cases' above and cf. also <yagh> 'I' v.23 (an apparently East Scandinavian form, cf. p.17); <hon> 'she' v.3; <ednar> 'her [gen. used as possessive]' v.22; <hedne> 'her [dat.]' v.22; <di> 'you [nom. pl., honorific use]' v.20 (a uniquely West Scandinavian form); <Dora> 'your [gen. pl. of same pronoun used as possessive]' v.20; <engin> 'no one [nom. m. sg.]' v.22.

Noun + possessive: <frinda sin> 'his kinsman' v.1; <Fong ednar> 'her arms' v.22.

There are few Scots loan-words in the *Hildina* ballad. In the eight verses cited, only <Yift> (< Scots *gif*?) seems a likely candidate.

> **Favoꝛ i ir i chimrie, Hel-**
> **leur ir i nam thite, gilla cof-**
> **dum thite cumma, veya**
> **thine mota vara goꝛt o yurn**
> **finna goꝛt i chimrie, ga vus**
> **da on da dalight bꝛow voꝛa,**
> **Firgive vus finna voꝛa fin**
> **vee Firgive findaꝛa mutha**
> **vus, lyv vus ye i tumtation,**
> **min deliveꝛa vus fro olt ilt,**
> **Amen.** Or **On fa meteth**
> **veꝛa.**

The Orkney Lord's Prayer.   *Reprinted from Wallace 1700:68-9*

The Orkney Lord's Prayer

Text:
Favor i ir i chimrie, Helleur ir i nam thite, gilla cosdum thite cumma,
veya thine mota vara gort o yurn sinna gort i chimrie, ga vus da on da
dalight brow vora, Firgive vus sinna vora sin vee Firgive sindara mutha
vus, lyv vus ye i tumtation, min delivera vus fro olt ilt, Amen. [Or:] On
sa meteth vera.

Rendboe (1989-90) provides facsimiles and texts of, as well as detailed
commentaries on, both the Orkney and Shetland versions of the Lord's
Prayer.

Although no more than a few lines, the Orkney Lord's Prayer exhibits a
number of the linguistic features outlined on pp.30-31.

Mood: <Firgive> 'forgive', indic.; <lyv> 'lead', imp.
Number: <nam> 'name'; <sinna> 'trespasses'.
Gender: <nam thite> 'thy name', n.; <veya thine> 'thy will', m.
Agreement: <dalight brow> 'daily bread', both words are n. sg.
Strong adjectives: <dalight> 'daily'; <olt> 'all'; <ilt> 'evil'.
Strong and weak nouns: <nam> 'name', strong; <veya> 'will', weak.
Voice: <Firgive> 'forgive', active; <vara gort> 'be done', passive.
Suffixed definite article: <yurn> [i.e. yur-n] 'the earth'.
Infinitive ends in a vowel: <vara> 'be'.

48

Scandinavian pronouns: <thine> 'thy', m. sg. possessive; <thite> 'thy', n. sg. possessive; <vee> 'we' (an apparently East Scandinavian form /vi:/, cf. p.17); <vus> 'us'; <vor> 'our', m. sg. possessive; <vora> 'our', f. pl. possessive.

Noun + possessive: <Favor> 'our father'; <nam thite> 'thy name'; <sinna vora> 'our trespasses'.

There is more evidence of interference from Scots here than in the *Hildina* ballad. The loan-words <tumtation> 'temptation' and <delivera> 'deliver' will be noted, as well as the spelling <nam> 'name' for Scandinavian *namn* or *navn* (though this latter may well be the responsibility of the collector). The Shetland version of the Lord's Prayer exhibits a yet greater number of loan-words. There <mutha> 'against' has become <gainst>, while the doxology, absent from the Orkney version, contains the words <puri> 'power' and <glori> 'glory'.

Fragments of Norn

The Unst rhyme

Text:

> De vare gue ti,
> when sone min guid to Kadanes:
> han kan ca' rossa mare
>   "   "   "   big bere
>   "   "   "   eld fire
>   "   "   "   klovandi taings.

Translation:
It was in a good hour that my son went to Caithness: He can call *rossa* 'mare', he can call *big* 'bere', he can call *eld* 'fire', he can call *klovan* 'di taings'.

The text above is as printed in Jakobsen (1928-32:xviii), but his special phonetic characters have been dispensed with since they are of no relevance for an understanding of the piece. A commentary in English is available in Rendboe 1984:68-79 (see p.24). The rhyme exhibits a mixture of Norn and Scots. It includes the Scots words <when>, <guid> and <ca> in addition to the four illustrating the son's linguistic proficiency; <to> may be Scots *to* or Norn *til* pronounced [tə]. Characteristically Scandinavian features, apart from the remaining vocabulary items, are the suffixed definite article in <klovan> 'the tongs', and the word-order noun + possessive in <sone min> 'my son'. According to Rendboe, nominative, accusative, genitive and dative are used in accordance with the original Common Scandinavian system, but that cannot be substantiated: <sone> (ON *sonr*) he declares nominative, while <gue> (ON *góðri*), with an identical ending, is deemed dative; <Kadanes> is said to be genitive, even though the basic form of this name must also have been *Kadanes*; <big>, <eld> and <klovan> are judged accusative, but while <klovan> does indeed correspond to the ON acc. *klofann*, <big> and <eld> may simply be basic forms devoid of any ending; even Rendboe agrees that <rossa> cannot reflect ON acc. *hryssu*.

The Cunningsburgh phrase

Text:
Myrk in e Liora, Luce in e Liunga, Tim in e Guest in e geungna.

Translation:
Dark is(?) in [the] chimney, light still in [the] heather, the time is [right that] the guest is gone.

The 'phrase' was recorded by George Low, and is given here as it appears in the printed version of his *Tour* (1879:180). A commentary in English is available in Rendboe 1993.

The words <Myrk> and <Luce> may be nouns or adjectives, but if the latter, they lack the neuter ending *-t* (cf. Faroese: *myrkt er* 'dark is [i.e., it is dark]'). The interpretation of the first half of the phrase offered here is uncertain (particularly the suggestion that <in e> represents both *er i* 'is in' and *enn í* 'still in'), but the second half is likely to be a reflex of ON: *Tíminn er, gestrinn er genginn*.

Fragments of conversation

Texts:
(1) Sponna ligere glegan.
(2) Mader to de bjadni.
(3) To lag de kjøren.
(4) Jarta, bodena komena rontena Komba.

Translations:
(1) The spoon is lying in the window.
(2) Food for the child.
(3) To move the cows.
(4) My dear, the boat has come round de Kaim [a hill in Foula].

All four fragments are taken from Jakobsen 1928-32:xcii (once again the special phonetic characters are replaced by ordinary letters). They seem to show the progressive deterioration of Scandinavian grammar. The structure of (1) is still recognisably Scandinavian, with suffixed definite articles in <Sponna> 'the spoon' and <glegan> 'the window' (the first, though, exhibiting an aberrant form), and a present-tense verb ending in *-er*. (2) has retained the nom. m. sg. *-er* ending in <Mader> 'food', but has a preposed Scots as well as a Scandinavian suffixed definite article in <de bjadni> 'the child'. (3) exhibits a similar hybrid construction in <de kjøren> 'the cows', and has in addition in <To lag> 'to move' a Scots infinitive marker and infinitive. In (4) the grammatical system is neither Norn nor Scots; the utterance offers a good example of the levelling of endings under -(*en*)*a* characteristic of many of the 'Norn' fragments, especially those in verse. Lexically (4) is Norn, and on that basis could be classed as Scandinavian in its ultimate stage of decline in the Northern Isles (for a view that (4) is grammatically as well as lexically Norn, see Rendboe 1984:66-8). (1-3) are also almost entirely made up of Norn words, though <de> must be a form of the Scots definite article, while <to> is Scots *to* or, in (2), Norn *til* (cf. the Unst rhyme above).

NOTES

1. A phonetic transcription represents speech sounds on the principle that one symbol denotes one sound and one sound only. A phonemic transcription is similar, but broader. Here one symbol represents one distinctive speech sound, i.e. the smallest segment of sound that can distinguish two words. The /l/ in standard English *light*, for example, has a different sound from the /l/ in *pile* (and different symbols will be used to denote them in a phonetic transcription), but the two can never distinguish words because of their distribution: one occurs at the beginning of a word the other at the end. Thus in phonemic transcription, as above, /l/ suffices for both.

2. Inscriptions written in runes, an alphabetic form of writing developed by Germanic peoples around the beginning of the Christian era (for a good introduction to the topic, see Page 1987).

3. Also known as *i*-Umlaut, a vowel change which gives us, e.g., English *feet* (pl.) from *foot*, and the corresponding German *Füße* (pl.) from *Fuß*.

4. 'Rǫgnvaldr, Earl of Mœrir', now Møre, an area in north-western Norway.

5. There are several English translations of *Orkneyinga saga*; the most recent, by Hermann Pálsson and Paul Edwards, is cited in the bibliography. Also listed is the most readily available English edition of *Heimskringla* — a nineteenth-century version by Samuel Laing, revised in the 1960s. An English translation of *Historia Norwegiæ*, together with commentary, is in the course of publication by the Viking Society for Northern Research, London.

6. 'Haraldr finehair', King of Norway *c*. 860-930.

7. P-Celtic refers to one of the main branches of the Celtic language family, represented today by Welsh and Breton. The term P-Celtic derives from the occurrence of /p/ in words which in Q-Celtic (Irish and languages descended from it such as Scottish Gaelic) exhibit /k/, e.g. Welsh *pen* 'head', *pedwar* 'four', Irish *ceann*, *ceathair*.

8. Ogam is an epigraphic script invented by the Irish, probably in the third or fourth century A.D. It is based on a stem or reference line, on either side of or across which are scored a number of shorter lines at different angles to the stem, the combination of side, number and angle indicating the sound denoted (for a detailed account of the subject, see McManus 1991).

9. Scaldic verse is a distinct genre of Old Norse poetry. It was usually composed by named individuals, and has a highly elaborate structure including strict rhyme and metre. Its formal attributes have favoured the retention of the original wording (or something close to it) throughout centuries of recitation and copying. The most comprehensive edition of Scaldic verse remains Finnur

Jónsson 1912-15. Turville-Petre 1976 provides an introduction to the subject in English and includes a number of texts and translations

10. Drift refers to the joint inheritance by languages of features that predetermine them to develop in the same or a similar way.

11. Apocope denotes the loss of end syllables, metathesis (in the present instance) the interchange of position between sounds in a word.

12. Reverse spellings arise from the coalescence of sounds and resulting uncertainty about how words with the product of the coalescence should be written. If /o/, /o:/ had regularly become /u/, /u:/ in Northern-Isles Scandinavian, for example, but scribes knew that what they pronounced /u/ or /u:/ was sometimes traditionally written <o>, it is conceivable they might have inserted <o> in words which historically had always had /u/ or /u:/.

13. The resulting sounds were probably in a range between, roughly, English 'ch' in *church* and German 'ch' in *ich*.

14. Another Shetland Lord's Prayer has recently come to light, said to be from Unst and to date from about 1800 (Rendboe 1989:81, 83-5). It adds little or nothing of linguistic significance, however, and in any case looks as though it may ultimately be dependent on Low's version.

15. English prose translations of all three poems can be found in Vigfusson and Powell 1883:302-8, 341-5, 363-9. *Krákumál* has also been put into English verse (Schlauch 1930:259-67). For a recent discussion of the late flowering of Scaldic verse in Orkney, see Hermann Pálsson 1984.

16. In progressive *i*-mutation [j] causes a following back vowel to adopt front articulation; thus [ja] can become [je], contrast Old Norse (and Icelandic) *jafn* 'even', Faroese *javn* with Danish *jævn*, Swedish *jämn*.

17. Long consonants have prolonged articulation, as for example in Italian.

18. Because of the difficulties involved in establishing even a rudimentary phonology of Norn (cf. Barnes 1991:433-9), the brief survey offered here focuses on morphological features, which by and large are the easiest to recognise. Norn phonology clearly had its origins in Germanic and Old Norse, but many of the details of its development elude us (cf., however, the remarks on pp.13-21, and Barnes 1984:357-9).

19. Transliteration involves the replacing of the letters of one script by those of another, and nothing further. Thus the runic inscriptions reproduced here in bold type appear exactly as in the original save only that the runes have been converted into equivalents in the roman alphabet. (On the problems and practice of transliteration from runic to roman, see Barnes 1994:12-15. Important conventions to be noted are:] [= lacuna of unknown length at start/end of line; * = unreadable but countable runes; ... = unreadable and uncountable runes; ( ) = uncertain runes or dividers.)

BIBLIOGRAPHY

Baldwin, John R. 1984. 'Hogin and Hametoun: Thoughts on the stratification of a Foula *tun*.' In: Barbara E. Crawford (ed.), *Essays in Shetland History*. Lerwick: The Shetland Times Ltd., 33-64.

Ballantyne, John H., and Brian Smith 1994. *Shetland Documents 1580-1611*. Lerwick: Shetland Islands Council & The Shetland Times Ltd.

Ballantyne, John H., and Brian Smith forthcoming. *Shetland Documents 1195-1579*.

Barnes, Michael 1984. 'Orkney and Shetland Norn.' In: Peter Trudgill (ed.), *Language in the British Isles*. Cambridge: Cambridge University Press, 352-66.

Barnes, Michael P. 1989. 'The death of Norn.' In: Heinrich Beck (ed.), *Germanische Rest- und Trümmersprachen*. Berlin: de Gruyter, 21-43.

Barnes, Michael P. 1991a. 'Norwegian, Norn, Icelandic or West Norse? The language of the Maeshowe inscriptions.' In: John Ole Askedal *et al.* (eds.), *Festskrift til Ottar Grønvik på 75-årsdagen den 21. oktober 1991*. Oslo: Universitetsforlaget, 70-87.

Barnes, Michael P. 1991b. 'Reflections on the structure and the demise of Orkney and Shetland Norn.' In: P. Sture Ureland and George Broderick (eds.), *Language Contact in the British Isles* (Linguistische Arbeiten 238). Tübingen: Niemeyer, 429-60.

Barnes, Michael P. 1993. 'Towards an edition of the Scandinavian runic inscriptions of the British Isles: some thoughts', *Northern Studies* 29 (1992), 32-42.

Barnes, Michael P. 1994. *The Runic Inscriptions of Maeshowe, Orkney* (Runrön 8). Uppsala: Institutionen för nordiska språk.

Barnes, Michael P. 1996. 'Jakob Jakobsen and the Norn language of Shetland.' In: Doreen J. Waugh (ed.), *Shetland's Northern Links: Language and History*. Edinburgh: Scottish Society for Northern Studies, 1-15.

Barnes, Michael, and R.I. Page 1996. 'Two runic inscriptions from the Northern Isles', *Nytt om runer* 10 (1995), 12-13.

Bjarni Aðalbjarnarson 1941. *Heimskringla* I (Íslenzk fornrit XXVI). Reykjavík: Hið íslenzka fornritafélag.

Brøgger, A.W. 1930. *Den norske bosetningen på Shetland-Orknøyene* (Skrifter utgitt av Det Norske Videnskaps-Akademi i Oslo. II. Hist.-Filos. Klasse. 1930. No. 3). Oslo.

Campbell, J.L. 1954. 'The Norse language in Orkney in 1725', *Scottish Historical Review* 33, 175.

Catford, J.C. 1957. 'Shetland dialect', *Shetland Folk Book* 3, 71-5.

Chapman, Kenneth G. 1962. *Icelandic-Norwegian Linguistic Relationships* (*Norsk tidsskrift for sprogvidenskap* Supplement vol. VII). Oslo: Universitetsforlaget.

Collingwood, W.G. 1908. 'The ballad of Hildina', *Old-Lore Miscellany of Orkney Shetland Caithness and Sutherland* I, 211-16 (= Old Lore Series 6).

Crawford, Barbara E. 1987. *Scandinavian Scotland* (Scotland in the Early Middle Ages 2). Leicester University Press.

Dickins, Bruce 1966-9. 'An Orkney scholar: Hugh Marwick 1881-1965', *Saga-Book of the Viking Society* XVII, 1-17.

DN = Chr. C.A. Lange *et al.*, *Diplomatarium Norvegicum* I-XXII (1849 in progress). Christiania/Kristiania/Oslo: Malling/Kommisjonen for Diplomatarium Norvegicum.

Dorian, Nancy C. 1981. *Language Death*. Philadelphia: University of Pennsylvania Press.

Dressler, Wolfgang, and Ruth Wodak-Leodolter (eds.) 1977. *Language Death* (*International Journal of the Sociology of Language* 12).

Einar Ól. Sveinsson 1954. *Brennu-Njáls saga* (Íslenzk fornrit XII). Reykjavík: Hið íslenzka fornritafélag.

Edmondston, Arthur 1809. *A View of the Ancient and Present State of the Zetland Islands...* II. Edinburgh: Ballantyne.

Falk, Hjalmar, and Alf Torp 1900. *Dansk-norskens syntax*. Kristiania: Aschehoug.

Fellows-Jensen, Gillian 1984. 'Viking settlement in the Northern and Western Isles — the place-name evidence as seen from Denmark and the Danelaw.' In: Alexander Fenton and Hermann Pálsson (eds.), *The Northern and Western Isles in the Viking World*. Edinburgh: John Donald, 148-68.

Finnbogi Guðmundsson 1965. *Orkneyinga saga* (Íslenzk fornrit XXXIV). Reykjavík: Hið íslenzka fornritafélag.

Finnur Jónsson 1912-15. *Den norsk-islandske skjaldedigtning* A I, B I, 800-1200, A II, B II, 1200-1400 (4 vols., reprinted 1967-73). København: Gyldendal.

Flom, George T. 1928-9. 'The transition from Norse to Lowland Scotch in Shetland, 1600-1850', *Saga-Book of the Viking Society* X, 145-64.

Forsyth, Katherine forthcoming. 'Language in Pictland: The case against non-Indo-European Pictish.' Third A.G. Van Hamel Lecture 1995.

Geipel, John 1971. *The Viking Legacy*. Newton Abbot: David and Charles.

Goudie, Gilbert 1904. *The Celtic and Scandinavian Antiquities of Shetland*. Edinburgh: Blackwood.

Grønneberg, Roy 1981. *Jakobsen and Shetland*. Lerwick: Shetland Publishing.

Hagland, Jan Ragnar 1993. 'Two runic inscriptions from Orphir, Orkney.' In: Colleen E. Batey *et al.* (eds.), *The Viking Age in Caithness, Orkney and the North Atlantic*. Edinburgh: Edinburgh University Press, 370-74.

Hermann Pálsson 1984. 'A florilegium in Norse from medieval Orkney.' In: Alexander Fenton and Hermann Pálsson (eds.), *The Northern and Western Isles in the Viking World*. Edinburgh: John Donald, 258-64.

Hermann Pálsson and Paul Edwards 1978. *Orkneyinga saga: The History of the Earls of Orkney*. London: Hogarth Press.

Holder-Egger, O. 1887. *Vita Findani*. *Monvmenta Germaniae historica scriptorvm* XV:1, 502-6. Hannoverae.

Hreinn Benediktsson 1972. *The First Grammatical Treatise* (University of Iceland Publications in Linguistics 1). Reykjavík: Institute of Nordic Linguistics.

Hægstad, Marius 1900. *Hildinakvadet* (Videnskabsselskabets Skrifter. II. Historisk-filosofiske Klasse. 1900. No. 2). Christiania.

Indrebø, Gustav 1951. *Norsk målsoga* (ed. Per Hovda and Per Thorson). Bergen: John Grieg.

Jackson, K.H. 1980. 'The Pictish language.' (See Wainwright 1980:129-66.)

Jakobsen, Jakob 1928-32. *An Etymological Dictionary of the Norn Language in Shetland* (2 vols., reprinted 1985). London/Copenhagen: David Nutt/Vilhelm Prior.

Jakobsen, Jakob 1936. *The Place-Names of Shetland* (reprinted 1993). London/Copenhagen: David Nutt/Vilhelm Prior.

König, Ekkehard and Johan van der Auwera (eds.) 1994. *The Germanic Languages.* London: Routledge.

Laing, Samuel 1961. *Snorri Sturluson, Heimskringla: Sagas of the Norse Kings* (rev. P. Foote). London: Dent.

Laing, Samuel 1964. *Snorri Sturluson, Heimskringla: The Olaf Sagas* (rev. J. Simpson, 2 vols.). London: Dent.

Lamb, Raymond G. 1993. 'Carolingian Orkney and its transformation.' In: Colleen E. Batey *et al.* (eds.), *The Viking Age in Caithness, Orkney and the North Atlantic.* Edinburgh: Edinburgh University Press, 260-71.

Low, George 1879. *A Tour through the Islands of Orkney and Schetland.* Kirkwall: William Peace.

Macalister, R.A.S. 1940. 'The inscriptions and language of the Picts.' In: John Ryan (ed.), *Essays and Studies Presented to Professor Eoin MacNeill, D.Litt., on the Occasion of his Seventieth Birthday May 15th, 1938.* Dublin: At the Sign of the Three Candles, 184-226.

Marwick, Hugh 1929. *The Orkney Norn.* London: Oxford University Press.

McManus, Damian 1991. *A Guide to Ogam.* Maynooth: An Sagart.

Melchers, Gunnel 1981. 'The Norn element in Shetland dialect today — a case of "never accepted" language death.' In: Eva Ejerhed and Inger Henrysson (eds.), *Tvåspråkighet* (Umeå Studies in the Humanities 36). Umeå: University of Umeå, 254-61.

Morris, Christopher D. 1990. 'Viking Orkney: A survey.' In: Colin Renfrew (ed.), *The Prehistory of Orkney* (2nd ed.). Edinburgh: Edinburgh University Press, 210-42.

Nicolaisen, W.F.H. 1986. *Scottish Place-Names* (3rd impression). London: Batsford.

Olsen, Magnus 1932. 'Orknø-norn og norrøn diktning på Orknøerne', *Maal og Minne* 1932, 137-53.

Olsen, Magnus 1954. 'Runic inscriptions in Great Britain, Ireland and the Isle of Man.' In: Haakon Shetelig (ed.), *Viking Antiquities in Great Britain and Ireland* VI. Oslo: Aschehoug, 151-233.

OSR = Alfred W. Johnston and Amy Johnston 1907-13. *Orkney and Shetland Records* 1. London: Viking Society.

Page, R.I. 1987. *Runes.* London: British Museum.

Pettersen, Egil 1988. 'Orknøynorn eller svensk?', *Maal og Minne* 1988, 190-98.

Rendboe, Laurits 1984. 'How "worn out" or "corrupted" was Shetland Norn in its final stage?', *NOWELE* 3, 53-88.

Rendboe, Laurits 1985. *The Shetland Literary Tradition* (2 parts, Introduction and Anthology; also dated 1986). Odense: Odense University.

Rendboe, Laurits 1987. *Det gamle shetlandske sprog* (*NOWELE* Supplement vol. 3). Odense Universitetsforlag.

Rendboe, Laurits 1989-90. 'The Lord's Prayer in Orkney and Shetland Norn 1-2', *NOWELE* 14, 77-112; 15, 49-111.

Rendboe, Laurits 1993. 'Low's last local Norn text from Shetland 1774', *NOWELE* 21/22, 117-36.

Rindler-Schjerve, Rosita 1989. 'Sprachverschiebung und Sprachtod: funktionelle und strukturelle Aspekte.' In: Heinrich Beck (ed.), *Germanische Rest- und Trümmersprachen*. Berlin: de Gruyter, 1-14.

Ritchie, Anna 1990. 'Orkney in the Pictish kingdom.' In: Colin Renfrew (ed.), *The Prehistory of Orkney* (2nd ed.). Edinburgh: Edinburgh University Press, 183-204.

Rivet, A.L.F., and Colin Smith 1979. *The Place-Names of Roman Britain*. London: Batsford.

Sandison, William (ed.) 1953. *Shetland Verse: Remnants of the Norn*. Shrewsbury: Wilding & Son.

Schlauch, Margaret 1930. *The Saga of the Volsungs. The Saga of Ragnar Lodbrok, together with The Lay of Kraka* (3rd ed. 1964). London: American-Scandinavian Foundation/Allen & Unwin.

Schmidt, Annette 1985. *Young People's Dyirbal: An Example of Language Death from Australia* (Cambridge Studies in Linguistics supplementary volume). Cambridge: Cambridge University Press.

Scott, Hew 1928. *Fasti Ecclesiæ Scoticanæ* (new ed.) VII. Edinburgh: Tweeddale Court.

Seip, Didrik Arup 1955. *Norsk språkhistorie til omkring 1370* (2nd ed.). Oslo: Aschehoug.

Sibbald, Sir Robert 1845. *Description of the Islands of Orkney and Zetland* (reprinted from the edition of 1711). Edinburgh: Thomas Stevenson.

Smith, Brian 1990. 'Shetland, Scandinavia, Scotland, 1300-1700: the changing nature of contact.' In: Grant G. Simpson (ed.), *Scotland and Scandinavia 800-1800*. Edinburgh: John Donald, 25-37.

Smith, Brian 1996. 'The development of the spoken and written Shetland dialect: a historian's view.' In: Doreen J. Waugh (ed.), *Shetland's Northern Links: Language and History*. Edinburgh: Scottish Society for Northern Studies, 30-43.

Stewart, John 1953. 'Shetland verse' (review of Sandison 1953), *The New Shetlander* 37, 20-21.

Stewart, John 1964. 'Norn in Shetland', *Fróðskaparrit* 13, 158-75.

Stewart, John 1970. 'Place-names of Fula', *Fróðskaparrit* 18, 307-19.

Stewart, John 1987. *Shetland Place-Names*. Lerwick: Shetland Library and Museum.

Storm, Gustav 1880. *Monumenta Historica Norvegiæ*. Kristiania.

Thomson, William P.L., and Christine J. Omand 1986. 'St Findan and the Pictish-Norse transition.' In: R.J. Berry and H.N. Firth (eds.), *The People of Orkney* (Aspects of Orkney 4). Kirkwall: Orkney Press, 279-87.

Tierney, J.J. 1967. *Dicuili liber de mensura orbis terrae* (Scriptores Latini Hiberniae VI). Dublin: Institute for Advanced Studies.

Turville-Petre, E.O.G. 1976. *Scaldic Poetry*. Oxford: Clarendon Press.

Vigfusson, Gudbrand, and F. York Powell 1883. *Corpvs Poeticvm Boreale. The Poetry of the Old Northern Tongue from the Earliest Times to the Thirteenth Century* II (Court Poetry). Oxford: Clarendon Press.

Wainwright, F.T. 1962. 'The Scandinavian settlement.' In: F.T. Wainwright (ed.), *The Northern Isles*. Edinburgh: Nelson, 117-62.

Wainwright, F.T. (ed.) 1980. *The Problem of the Picts* (2nd ed.). Perth: Melven Press.

Wallace, James 1700. *An Account of the Islands of Orkney*. London: Jacob Tonson.

Aasen, Ivar 1848. *Det norske Folksprogs Grammatik*. Kristiania: Det kongelige norske Videnskabs-Selskab.

THE AUTHOR

M ichael P. Barnes, born in 1940, took a BA Degree in Scandinavian Languages at University College London in 1963, followed by an MA in the same field in 1966. As well as London, he has studied in Norway, Sweden and the Faroes. Since 1964 he has taught in the Department of Scandinavian Studies, University College London, where he is currently Professor of Scandinavian Studies.

Michael Barnes has published books and articles on Scandinavian-language topics, including most recently *The Runic Inscriptions of Maeshowe, Orkney* (1994), *The Runic Inscriptions of Viking Age Dublin* (1997 – co-authored by J. R. Hagland and R. I. Page), and the chapter on Faroese in the reference work *The Germanic Languages* (1994). He was for many years editor of *Saga-Book*, the journal of the Viking Society for Northern Research, and is currently the society's joint honorary secretary.